# KETO AND MENOPAUSE

THE COMPLETE KETOGENIC DIET WITH 200 TASTY RECIPES TO HELP YOU OVERCOME MENOPAUSE ISSUES, REGAIN YOUR VITALITY, AND LIVE THIS MOMENT OF YOUR LIFE IN THE HEALTHIEST AND PROPER WAY

## KETY WOMACK

# TABLE OF CONTENTS

# INTRODUCTION

*T*he ketogenic diet may offer benefits for women during menopause, including increased insulin sensitivity, decreased weight gain, and reduced cravings.

*Dealing with weight issues can be disheartening, and you do not have to be extremely overweight or obese to feel the effects. These extra pounds can put a strain on your overall health and wellness. They can make you less efficient in your work life and everyday activities and take you away from the things you like to do and the places you love to visit. Excess weight can take away your joy for living and prevent you from living life to the fullest.*

*Besides weight, when people get older, their bones weaken. At 50, your bones are likely not as strong as they used to be; however, you can keep them in really good conditions. Consuming milk to give calcium cannot do enough to strengthen your bones. What you*

*can do is to make use of the Keto diet as it is low in toxins. Toxins negatively affect the absorption of nutrients, and so with this, your bones can take in all they need.*

*The ketogenic diet is the ultimate tool you can use to plan your future. Can you picture being more involved, more productive and efficient, and more relaxed and energetic? That future is possible for you, and it does not have to be a complicated process to achieve that vision. You can choose right now to be healthier and slimmer, and more fulfilled tomorrow. It is possible with the ketogenic diet.*

# 1. THE KETO DIET MINDSET

Like any other life-transforming endeavor, the keto diet regimen is dependent on your mindset. You must be prepared to face the emotional, physical, and psychological obstacles that will arise in the course of achieving your goals. This underpins the impact the diet will have on your life. In this regard, one of the fundamental elements of keto is a mindset that is equipped to deal with many obstacles and challenges.

For some, the desire to lose weight is the underlying impetus, while others are motivated by the goal of living healthier lives. In some cases, a person may be forced to consider a diet change for medical or biological reasons. Regardless of the motivation, maintaining the right mindset always determines the success of a change in diet. In this regard, attaining an appropriate mindset is the first step towards initiating and benefitting from a keto-based diet.

## The Right Mindset for a Keto Diet

When beginning a keto diet, the first phase of your journey must be adopting an appropriate mindset that will allow you to make this lifestyle change successfully. While you might set your goals right from the start, you must consider that your energy and enthusiasm is likely to wane over time. For most people, this results in failure, which is then translated into frustration and the loss of confidence in the ketogenic diet. By emotionally and psychologically preparing oneself for the journey ahead, it is possible to achieve this feat quite easily.

You must first acknowledge and accept in your mind that the diet does work and that you can experience its impact on your life. This is the first and most crucial thought process that will help you actively and judiciously stick to the plan. If you have tried other diet plans in the past with little success, this particular thought process may be hard to come by. However, by shifting your focus to scientific and factual material regarding the diet, you may begin to appreciate its efficacy.

The capacity to individually internalize this concept forms the basis of the essential mindset for a keto diet. By eliminating any form of doubt in your mind with respect to the benefits and impact of a keto diet, you set yourself up for success. This is because it helps you stay focused on the outcome while ignoring the day to day challenges and distractions that will surely arise. Internalization and appreciation of the benefits and effectiveness of the keto diet create the necessary momentum needed to consistently adhere to the stipulations that come with the implementation of the diet.

The elimination of excuses is also fundamental if you are to realize the benefits of a keto diet. For most people, dietary changes are seen as major transformations that occur overnight. For a woman in her 50s, this can prove daunting and even scary. When you have already lived on a different diet for half a century, you have an internal block that causes you to doubt your ability to change the content of your diet. You are likely to come up with numerous excuses and justifications as to why such a diet may not work for you. If you are looking at a keto diet as a total overhaul of how you are a person, then there is a higher likelihood you will find the endeavor too arduous even to try.

By holding onto the notion, a keto diet is only successful when drastic and dramatic changes are made in your life, you hold yourself back with your own thoughts. In most cases, this line of thought should raise the red flag of fear and unnecessary excuses. While such notions may have been informed by your former attempts at dieting, it is important that you approach a keto diet with a fresh and inquisitive mind.

It is also important to approach the keto diet as a new partner that will bring you much-awaited love, compassion, and care. In other words, you have to understand and appreciate the fact the keto diet is there to transform your life like never before. In this case, therefore, you must assume a sense of self-love and care to ensure that it works. Day-to-day interactions and experiences can often impose a sense of negativity and self-loathing. In failing to accomplish various goals, meet specific demands, or accomplish certain personal, professional, or social goals, the burden of guilt and self-hate is likely to emerge.

Such a state of mind is limited in numerous ways, and as such, it cannot achieve the desired frequency of caring for itself. Once you learn to be kind and patient with yourself, you realize life has its ups and downs. Regardless of these challenges, you must give yourself the time and space to fail, learn, and grow as you go. The self-care mindset is crucial for effectiveness on the keto diet. By appreciating and loving yourself, you initiate a process in which your well-being is paramount to your survival, and as such, you are ready to undertake any efforts whatsoever to improve the quality of your life. A sense of purpose and limitlessness becomes a constant aspect of your life, and as such, you are able to see your goals and ambitions through.

As is the case, with most new things, encounters, and experiences, you are likely to feel the need to remind yourself of the feeling continuously. For instance, when you buy a new phone, you may not want to put it down even as you explore its features and quirks. Over time your adoration for the new item may turn into an obsession or compulsive behavior that can be hard to break. The same analogy works when it comes to dieting. In setting out to try a new diet, as is the case with a keto diet, you may fixate on the expected outcomes and results.

It is important to note the fact that while your weight may be slow to change, there is a likelihood your muscle structure will have a change in terms of getting leaner. By moving away from the metric-tracking mentality, you allow yourself the time to acclimate to the diet and notice the overall changes it brings about in your physical, psychological, and emotional well-being rather than fixating on the pounds lost or gained.

Cognitively preparing for the long-haul is also vital in achieving the goals and benefits of a keto diet.

The best way to appreciate a ketogenic diet is by looking at it as a lifestyle change rather than a change in dietary intake. While the benefits of the diet are factual and well documented, they take time to come about. Most people, however, hold the belief that a keto diet is a quick fix solution that allows them to transform their health, weight, and body shape within weeks or months. Having gleaned information from various media platforms, such individuals are quick to adopt the diet with the hope of having an overnight transformation.

The quick-fix mindset is one of the surest ways of failing in your pursuit to experience the benefits of a ketogenic diet. You must be willing to endure for the long-term goals while celebrating the short-term gains. A two-week on a two-month keto diet may accord you the much needed weight loss. However, such changes are likely to disappear just as fast in the absence of long-term commitment.

**Strategies to Develop the Right Mindset for a Keto Diet**

Having understood the dynamics surrounding the perfect keto diet mindset, you may wonder how you will achieve such a feat. In other words, you want to establish the actual and practical steps towards developing a paradigm shift. The fields of psychology and behavioral science have been instrumental in expanding knowledge and information surrounding human behavior.

- Being aware of your inner and outer surrounding

In this regard, the first and most important strategy is raising one's awareness of both inner and outer surroundings. With food as a crucial trigger of behavior and habit, maintaining a sense of awareness regarding your thought patterns, cravings, and moment to moment activities offer the first step towards mastering your dietary behavior.

In an effort to build upon your awareness, you might need to keep a journal as one way of keeping track of your thought patterns and activities. With this in place, it becomes easier to review your day while noticing recurrent thoughts and activities. This will prove crucial in helping you plan your day with respect to meals and exercises while keeping track of your dietary intake. Most importantly, however, is the fact it will help you in cultivating the discipline needed with respect to keeping track of your consumption patterns.

- Keeping an open mind

With your awareness in check, you will need to strive to have an open mind considering the diverse results of the keto diet from one person to another. In an effort to establish a keto-diet mindset, it will be imperative that you remain as open as possible to new ideas, experiments, lessons, disappointments, and victories. Having a fixed mindset regarding the outcomes and expectations from a keto diet serves no purpose at all. You should not approach a keto diet experience with pre-established ideas and notions.

- The willingness to put in the work

While most media depictions of keto diets revolve around quick and short-term gains associated with the change, the reality is far more arduous and long. Beyond the glamour of abs, swift loss of weight, and bright and glowing skin, you must be willing to invest your time and resources to realize your health and diet goals. This translates to creating time to educate yourself and gain the knowledge and skills necessary to actualize your keto diet dream.

- The readiness to make changes in your life

The attainment of a keto diet mindset is also contingent upon your ability to make changes across various areas of your life. Having appreciated food and eating as habitual behaviors, you must be willing to overcome and transform various aspects of your life if you are to enjoy the benefits of a keto diet. This requires a comprehensive audit of your life with a focus on your habits and behavior over time. Your ability to change primarily lies in your comprehension of the factors around your day-to-day life.

As you work towards achieving your healthy diet goal, the need for change will arise from every other corner. Any form of resistance from any faculty of your life may result in unprecedented outcomes with respect to your dieting. In essence, in committing to a keto diet, you must be ready to endure various uncomfortable experiences in the short-term.

- Visualization

Visualization entails creating mental images of yourself in a healthier, leaner, and more confident state. This means taking time to capture all the upsides that will result from your efforts to transform yourself. You will need to look at the type of relationships you will have, the health benefits associated with the changes you make, and most importantly, what it will take for you to achieve your goals. Engaging in this exercise is vital with respect to emotionally and psychologically preparing yourself for the benefits, as well as the responsibility needed to achieve your goal.

# 2. BENEFITS AND RISKS OF THE KETO DIET

**B**enefits of a Ketogenic Diet
**Reduction of Cravings and Appetite**

Many people gain weight simply because they cannot control their cravings and appetite for caloric foods. The ketogenic diet helps eliminate these problems, but it does not mean that you will never be hungry or want to eat. You will feel hungry but only when you have to eat. Several studies have shown that the less carbohydrates you eat, the less you eat overall. Eating healthier foods that are high in fat helps reduce your appetite, as you lose more weight faster on a low-fat diet. The reason for this is that low carbohydrate diets help lower insulin levels, as your body does not need too much insulin to convert glycogen to glucose while eliminating excess water in your body. This diet helps you reduce visceral fat. In this way, you will get a slimmer look and shape. It is the most difficult fat to lose, as it surrounds the organs as it increases. High doses can cause inflammation and insulin resistance. Coconut oil can produce an immediate source of energy as it increases ketone levels in your body.

## Reduction of Risk of Heart Disease

Triglycerides, fat molecules in your body, have close links with heart disease. They are directly proportional as the more the number of triglycerides, the higher your chances of suffering from heart disease. You can reduce the number of free triglycerides in your body by reducing the number of carbohydrates, as is in the keto diets.

## Reduces Chances of Having High Blood Pressure

Weight loss and blood pressure have a close connection; thus, since you are losing weight while on the keto diet, it will affect your blood pressure.

## Fights Type 2 Diabetes

Type two diabetes develops as a result of insulin resistance. This is a result of having huge amounts of glucose in your system, with the keto diet this is not a possibility due to the low carbohydrate intake.

## Increases the Production of HDL

High-density lipoprotein is referred to as good cholesterol. It is responsible for caring calories to your liver, thus can be reused. High fat and low carbohydrate diets increase the production of HDL in your body, which also reduces your chances of getting a heart disease. Low-density lipoprotein is referred to as bad cholesterol.

## Suppresses Your Appetite

It is a strange but true effect of the keto diet. It was thought that this was a result of the production of ketones but this was proven wrong as a study taken between people on a regular balanced diet and some on the keto diet and their appetites were generally the same. It, however, helps to suppress appetite as it is it has a higher fat content than many other diets. Food stays in the stomach for longer as fat and is digested slowly, thus provides a sense of fullness. On top of that, proteins promote the secretion of cholecystokinin, which is a hormone that aids in regulating appetite. It is also believed that the ketogenic diet helps to suppress your appetite by continuous blunting of appetite. There is increased appetite in the initial stages of the diet, which decreases over time.

## Changes in Cholesterol Levels

This is kind of on the fence between good and bad. This is because the ketogenic diet involves a high fat intake which makes people wonder about the effect on blood lipids and its potential to increase chances of heart disease and strokes, among others. Several major components play a lead role in determining this, which is: LDL, HDL, and blood triglyceride levels. Heart disease correlates with high levels of LDL and cholesterol. On the other hand, high levels of HDL are seen as protection from diseases caused by cholesterol levels. The impacts of the diet on cholesterol are not properly known. Some research has shown that there is no change in cholesterol levels while others have said that there is change. If you stay in deep ketosis for a very long period of time, your blood lipids will increase, but you will have to go through some negative effects of the ketogenic diet which will be corrected when the diet is over. If a person does not remain following the diet strictly for like ten years, he/she will not experience any cholesterol problems. It is difficult to differentiate the difference between diet and weight loss in general. The effect of the ketogenic diet on cholesterol has been boiled down to if you lose fat on the ketogenic diet then your cholesterol levels will go down, and if you don't lose fat, then your cholesterol levels will go up. Strangely, women have a larger cholesterol level addition than men, while both are on a diet. As there is no absolute conclusion on the effect of the ketogenic diet on cholesterol, you are advised to have your blood lipid levels constantly checked for any bad effects. Blood lipid levels should be checked before starting the diet and about eight weeks after starting. If repeated results show a worsening of lipid levels, then you should abandon the diet or substitute saturated fats with unsaturated fats.

# Risks of a Ketogenic Diet

## Low Energy Levels

When available, the body prefers to use carbohydrates for fuel as they burn more effectively than fats. General drop-in energy level is a concern raised by many dieters due to the lack of carbohydrates. Studies have shown that it causes orthostatic hypotension which causes lightheadedness. It has come to be known that these effects can be avoided by providing enough supplemental nutrients like sodium. Many of the symptoms can be prevented by providing 5grams of sodium per day. Most times, fatigue disappears after a few weeks or even days, if fatigue doesn't disappear, then you should add a small number of carbohydrates to the diet as long as ketosis is maintained. The diet is not recommended when caring out high-intensity workouts, weight training, or high-intensity aerobic exercise as carbohydrates are an absolute requirement but are okay for low-intensity exercise.

## Effects on the Brain

It causes increased use of ketones by the brain. The increased use of ketones, among other reasons, result in the treating of childhood epilepsy. As a result of the changes that occur, the concern over the side effects, including permanent brain damage and short-term memory loss, has been raised. The origin of these concerns is difficult to understand. The brain is powered by ketones in the absence of glucose. Ketones are normal energy sources and not toxic as the brain creates enzymes, during fetal growth, that helps us use them. Epileptic children, though not the perfect examples, show some insight into the effects of the diet on the brain in the long term. There is no negative effect in terms of cognitive function. There is no assurance that the diet cannot have long term dietary effects, but no information proves that there are any negative effects. Some people feel they can concentrate more when on the ketogenic diet, while others feel nothing but fatigue. This is a result of differences in individual physiology. There are very few studies that vaguely address the point on short term memory loss. This wore off with the continuation of the study.

## Kidney Stones and Kidney Damage

As a result of the increased workload from having to filter ketones, urea, and ammonia, as well as dehydration concerns of the potential for kidney damage or passing kidney stones have been raised. The high protein nature of the ketogenic diet raises the alarms of individuals who are concerned with potential kidney damage. There is very little information that points to any negative effects of the diet on kidney function or the development of kidney stones. There is a low incidence of small kidney stones in epileptic children this may be as a result of the state of deliberate dehydration that the children are put at instead of the ketosis state itself. Some short term research shows no change in kidney function or increased incidents of kidney stones either after they are off the diet or after six months on a diet. There is no long-term data on the effects of ketosis on kidney function; thus, no complete conclusions can be made. People with preexisting kidney issues are the only ones who get problems from high protein intake. From an unscientific point of view, one would expect increased incidents of this to happen to athletes who consume very high protein diets, but it has not happened. This suggests that high protein intake, under normal conditions, is not harmful to the kidneys. To limit the possibility of kidney stones, it is advised to drink a lot of water to maintain hydration. For people who are predisposed to kidney stones should have their kidney function should be monitored to ensure that no complications arise if they decide to follow through with the diet.

## Constipation

A common side effect of the diet is reduced bowel movements and constipation. This arises from two different causes: lack of fiber and gastrointestinal absorption of foods. First, the lack of carbs in the diet means that unless supplements are taken, fiber intake is low. Fiber is very important to our systems. High fiber intake can prevent some health conditions, including heart disease and some forms of cancer. Use some type of sugar-free fiber supplement to prevent any health problems and help you maintain regular bowel movements. The diet also reduces the volume of stool due to enhanced absorption and digestion of food; thus, fewer waste products are generated.

## Fat Regain

Dieting, in general, has very low long term success rates. There are some effects of getting out of a ketogenic diet like the regain of fat lost through calorific restriction alone. This is true for any diet based on calorific restriction. It is expected for weight to be regained after carb reintroduction. For people who use the weighing scale to measure their success, they may completely shun carbs as they think it is the main reason for the weight regain. You should understand that most of the initial weight gain is water and glycogen.

## Immune System

There is a large variety in the immunity system response to ketogenic diets on different people. There has been some repost on reduction on some ailments such allergies and increased minor sickness susceptibility.

## Optic Neuropathy

This is optic nerve dysfunction. It has appeared in a few cases, but it is still existence. It was linked to the people not getting adequate amounts of calcium or vitamin supplements for about a year. All the cases were corrected by supplementation of adequate vitamin B, especially thiamine.

# 3. HOW THE KETOGENIC DIET CAN AID WITH THE SIGNS AND SYMPTOMS OF AGEING AND MENOPAUSE DIET

For ageing women, menopause will bring severe changes and challenges, but the ketogenic diet can help you switch gears effortlessly to continue enjoying a healthy and happy life. Menopause can upset hormonal levels in women, which consequently affects brainpower and cognitive abilities. Furthermore, due to less production of estrogens and progesterone, your sex drive declines, and you suffer from sleep issues and mood problems. Let's have a look at how a ketogenic diet will help solve these side effects.

### Enhanced Cognitive Functions

Usually, the hormone estrogen ensures continuous flow of glucose into your brain. But after menopause, the estrogen levels begin to drop dramatically, so does the amount of glucose reaching the bran. As a result, your functional brainpower will start to deteriorate. However, by following the keto diet for women over 50, the problem of glucose intake is circumvented. This results in enhanced cognitive functions and brain activity.

### Hormonal Balance

Usually, women face major symptoms of menopause due to hormonal imbalances. The keto diet for women over 50 works by stabilizing these imbalances such as estrogen. This aids in experiencing fewer and bearable menopausal symptoms like hot flashes. The keto diet also balances blood sugar levels and insulin and helps in controlling insulin sensitivity.

### Intensified Sex Drive

The keto diet surges the absorption of vitamin D, which is essential for enhancing sex drive. Vitamin D ensures stable levels of testosterone and other sex hormones that could become unstable due to low levels of testosterone.

### Better Sleep

Glucose disturbs your blood sugar levels dramatically, which in turn leads to poor quality of sleep. Along with other menopausal symptoms, good sleep becomes a huge problem as you age. The keto diet for women over 50 not only balances blood glucose levels, but also stabilizes other hormones like cortisol, melatonin, and serotonin warranting an improved and better sleep.

## Reduces Inflammation

Menopause can upsurge the inflammation levels by letting potential harmful invaders in our system, which results in uncomfortable and painful symptoms. Keto diet for women over 50 uses the healthy anti-inflammatory fats to reduce inflammation and lower pain in your joints and bones.

## Fuel Your Brain

Are you aware that your brain is composed of 60% fat or more? This infers that it needs a larger amount of fat to keep it functioning optimally. In other words, the ketones from the keto diet serve as the energy source that fuels your brain cells.

## Nutrient Deficiencies

Ageing women tend to have higher deficiencies in essential nutrients such as, iron deficiency which leads to brain fog and fatigue; Vitamin B12 deficiency, which leads to neurological conditions like dementia; Fats deficiency, which can lead to problems with cognition, skin, vision; and Vitamin D deficiency that not only causes cognitive impairment in older adults and increase the risk of heart disease but also contribute to the risk of developing cancer. On a keto diet, the high-quality proteins ensure adequate and excellent sources of these important nutrients.

## Controlling Blood Sugar

Research has suggested a link between poor blood sugar levels and brain diseases such as Alzheimer's disease, Parkinson's disease, or Dementia. Some factors contributing to Alzheimer's disease may include:

- Enormous intake of carbohydrates, especially from fructose—which is drastically reduced in the ketogenic diet.

- Lack of nutritional fats and good cholesterol—which are copious and healthy in the keto diet

Keto diet helps control blood sugar and improve nutrition; which in turn not only improves insulin response and resistance but also protects against memory loss which is often a part of ageing.

# 4. GETTING STARTED WITH THE KETO DIET

We have talked about what is the ketogenic diet, its roots and usages and definitely its benefits when one gets into the metabolic state of ketosis. We will now leave the "why should you do it" behind for the time being and get started on "how should you do it."

We will be talking about the initial stages of how you should prepare yourself for the diet, what kind of foods you should be looking out for and what you should be expecting whilst on the diet and when you get into full blast ketosis. This is really the portion where you can use it to take action immediately and bring about the positive changes you are looking for.

**Step A: First Things First**

The most important thing to do before you start off is to take a moment to run through your mind if you have any outstanding physical ailments or problems, particularly if it were related to the gall bladder or liver. If you do not know, it might be a good idea to visit your physician for a full body checkup and let him or her know your intentions regarding taking the Keto route. Once he or she has given you the all-clear signal, you are free to begin your next steps. One thing to note though, do make sure your doctor already knows what the ketogenic diet is all about before you visit, else you might very well be making a wasted trip! If your doctor doesn't know, switch and find one who does.

Then, what you need to do is to calculate your daily macronutrient requirement with an ideal Keto diet that suits your requirement. As a beginner, I would suggest that you start off on the standard ketogenic diet (SKD) consisting of 75% fat, 20% proteins, and 5% carbs.

The following will help you get ready with a customized plan for a successful ketogenic diet:

• Find out your ideal body weight – For this, there are various calculators that are easily available wherein if you input your height, gender, and age, it will tell you what your ideal body weight should be. However, you need to know how the mechanics work, so we shall be looking at how to arrive at your ideal weight range using the body mass index (BMI) method.

Calculating your BMI using the metric system goes like this, weight in kilograms divided by height in meters squared. BMI using pounds and inches is pretty much the same, with your weight in pounds divided by height in inches squared, but you need to multiply the result with a conversion factor of 703. So if your weight is about 150 pounds and you have a height of about 5 foot 5 inches (65 inches), your BMI calculation goes like this 150 pounds divided by 65 inches squared, then multiplied by 703 (the conversion factor) to get 24.96.

The ideal range for BMI readings is between 18.5 to 24.9, which are classified as normal or healthy weight. Anything above or below this scale would not be desirable. As you can tell, there is a range for optimal weight, listen to what your body tells you as a good gauge.

- Find out your daily calorie requirement – This is important because it is the foundation for the later part of the breakup of macronutrients that you need for your daily diet. Though there are many, and I say many, online calculators that allow you to key your weight height and age to find out your daily calorie needs, over here, it is still the belief that you need to know how to get the numbers, so here we go!

For manual calculation of your daily calorie needs, we shall be using the method called the Mifflin-St Jeor formula. For men, the calculation goes like this

- 10 x weight (Kg) + 6.25 x height (cm) − 5 x age (years) + 5

So for a 30-year-old man who weighs 180 pounds (81.6kg) and stands at the height of 6 feet (183cm), his total daily intake should be 1,815 calories. For women, it is calculated below

- 10 x weight (Kg) + 6.25 x height (cm) − 5 x age (years) − 161

Similarly, for a 30-year-old lady who weighs 160 pounds (72.7kg) and measures 6 feet (183cm), her total daily intake will be 1,560 calories. Now that you know what your daily calorie intake should be, it is time for the fun part, knowing how to calculate your macronutrient breakdown. The fat's in the fire, to say the least!

- Find out the breakup of fats, carbs, and proteins to be included in your diet – This will help you understand how you can structure your meals so that you know that your daily dietary requirements are fulfilled correctly. We will need to know how many grams of fats, proteins and carbs that you will need.

Right now you already know how many calories per day you need, what is required now is the way to convert the calories to the macronutrient grams that makes it easier to track how much we are eating. So now, with an example of a 1,800 daily calories intake, when translated on the percentage requirements of the standard ketogenic diet of 75% fats, 20% protein and 5% carbs will give us 1,350 calories for fats, 360 calories for protein and 90 calories for carbohydrates.

The next step will be to divide up these calories by the caloric values that each gram of macronutrient yields. Both protein and carbohydrates give about 4 calories per gram while fats can provide 9 calories per gram. This says something about using fat as body fuel huh? So based on the example of 1,800 calories per day, the standard ketogenic diet will give a guideline of 150grams of fat, 90grams of protein and finally about 23grams of carbs.

This will give you a good idea of how many grams of macronutrients you need per day based on calorie intake. One thing to note is that whilst on a ketogenic diet, you generally do not need to count calories, because like what we have been saying all this while, eating a fat-based diet is very satiating and fulfilling. There are none of the hunger pangs that accompany most weight-loss diets nor the urges for food once you get fully Keto adapted. The guide here is to eat and listen to your body. Eat when hungry, to the point of fulfillment but not stuffing yourself, and you will find that the calories counting will take care of itself.

I would also like to state that when we are talking about carbs, we are just talking about that, and not net carbs. The concept of net carbs has been popularized where you take the total carbs and subtract the fiber content. Unfortunately, the net carbs idea is probably one of the main culprits why many think they are on the ketogenic diet yet fail to enjoy the benefits of nutritional ketosis. So treat carbs as carbs, and limit them to your daily macronutrient guideline.

- Items that you may need – At this juncture, we have talked plenty about nutritional ketosis and how it is good for you, but how do you know if you are indeed in a state of nutritional ketosis? This is where we need to talk about how ketones are measured and what are the tools you can use to measure them.

There are three types of ketone bodies that we are interested in

- Acetoacetate – the primary body found in urine

- Beta-hydroxybutyrate – the body found in the blood

- Acetone – the ketone body found in our breath

Due to cost and ease of use, testing for ketones found in the urine has been one of the more common ways to see if you are on your way to ketosis. However, testing via urine is largely imprecise. This is because the urine strips that are used to measure ketones are largely meant for people with diabetes who are testing for ketoacidosis, hence the strips are programmed to pick up larger doses of ketones. Also, as your body transits from burning sugar to fat, ketones are produced in larger amounts, hence when you first test for it via urine, it will be positive. However as your body starts absorbing the ketones for energy, moving into ketosis, less of it will be expelled via the urine. So there is a distinct possibility that as your body gets into nutritional ketosis, you wouldn't even know as the urine strips turn up negative results! Don't do this to yourself, it is very disheartening.

The other, more accurate way of testing for ketones would be via blood testing. This way is usually done via a prick of your finger for the blood to be dapped on the test strips for analysis using the blood ketone monitors. Ketosis is shown to be present when our blood ketone levels are around 1 to 3 millimolar per liter, with some measures going higher to 4 millimolar, so testing for ketosis using your blood is indeed the current most accurate way. However, the disposable strips used for testing are quite expensive, not to mention the matter of pricking yourself daily to check for blood ketone levels. I'm one such person who doesn't really fancy the pain, especially on a daily basis!

So what then for those who don't want blood testing? Fortunately, there is the option of breath testing, which measures the amount of acetone present in your breath using a breath monitor. Essentially you breathe or exhale for about 10 to 15 seconds to force out the air that is at the bottom of your lungs into the monitor. Breath ketone bodies have been found to be as reliably correlated as blood ketone bodies to nutritional ketosis. Personally, I am testing for ketosis using the Ketonix breath ketone monitor, since it just needs a hard blow and there is no pain. More importantly, the results are the same as blood ketone testing. At this point, I would like to bring a word in about testing for ketones using the police breathalyzers, where there has been some talk about it. I can only say, use the right tool for the uses it is meant to do, and considering the breathalyzers are about a third more expensive than ketonix, I reckon it better to just stick to that.

- Prep it slow or take the plunge – This segment will touch on how you want to begin your ketogenic journey. Remember we are essentially switching from being sugar burners to being fat burners when we phase into ketosis. This transition is not without its slight share of troubles. Imagine your body having gorged itself on glucose from all the carbs that you have been consuming for the past twenty or thirty years, and now all of a sudden, your body is going to be severely deprived of the glucose buffet, the consequence is very much like an addiction withdrawal.

# 5. COMMON MISTAKES TO AVOID

Do you feel like you are giving your all to the Keto diet but you still aren't seeing the results you want? You are measuring ketones, working out, and counting your macros, but you still aren't losing the weight you want. Here are the most common mistakes that most people make when beginning the Keto diet.

## Too Many Snacks

There are many snacks you can enjoy while following the Keto diet, like nuts, avocado, seeds, and cheese. But, snacking can be an easy way to get too many calories into the diet while giving your body an easy fuel source besides stored fat. Snacks need to be only used if you frequently hunger between meals. If you aren't extremely hungry, let your body turn to your stored fat for its fuel between meals instead of dietary fat.

## Not Consuming Enough Fat

The ketogenic diet isn't all about low carbs. It's also about high fats. You need to be getting about 75 percent of your calories from healthy fats, five percent from carbs, and 20 percent from protein. Fat makes you feel fuller longer, so if you eat the correct amount, you will minimize your carb cravings, and this will help you stay in ketosis. This will help your body burn fat faster.

## Consuming Excessive Calories

You may hear people say you can eat what you want on the Keto diet as long as it is high in fat. Even though we want that to be true, it is very misleading. Healthy fats need to make up the biggest part of your diet. If you eat more calories than what you are burning, you will gain weight, no matter what you eat because these excess calories get stored as fat. An average adult only needs about 2,000 calories each day, but this will vary based on many factors like activity level, height, and gender.

## Consuming a lot of Dairies

For many people, dairy can cause inflammation and keeps them from losing weight. Dairy is a combo food meaning it has carbs, protein, and fats. If you eat a lot of cheese as a snack for the fat content, you are also getting a dose of carbs and protein with that fat. Many people can tolerate dairy, but moderation is the key. Stick with no more than one to two ounces of cheese or cream at each meal. Remember to factor in the protein content.

## Consuming a lot of Protein

The biggest mistake that most people make when just beginning the Keto diet is consuming too much protein. Excess protein gets converted into glucose in the body called gluconeogenesis. This is a natural process where the body converts the energy from fats and proteins into glucose when glucose isn't available. When following a ketogenic diet, gluconeogenesis happens at different rates to keep body function. Our bodies don't need a lot of carbs, but we do need glucose. You can eat absolute zero carbs, and through gluconeogenesis, your body will convert other substances into glucose to be used as fuel. This is why carbs only make up five percent of your macros. Some parts of our bodies need carbs to survive, like kidneys, medulla, and red blood cells. With gluconeogenesis, our bodies make and stores extra glucose as glycogen just in case supplies become too low.

In a normal diet, when carbs are always available, gluconeogenesis happens slowly because the need for glucose is extremely low. Our body runs on glucose and will store excess protein and carbs as fat.

## Not Getting Enough Water

Water is crucial for your body. Water is needed for all your body does, and this includes burning fat. If you don't drink enough water, it can cause your metabolism to slow down, and this can halt your weight loss. Drinking 64 ounces or one-half gallon every day will help your body burn fat, flush out toxins, and circulate nutrients. When you are just beginning the Keto diet, you might need to drink more water since your body will begin to get rid of body fat by flushing it out through urine.

## Consuming Too Many Sweets

Some people might indulge in Keto brownies and Keto cookies that are full of sugar substitutes just because their net carb content is low, but you have to remember that you are still eating calories. Eating sweets might increase your carb cravings. Keto sweets are great on occasion; they don't need to be a staple in the diet.

## Not Getting Enough Sleep

Getting plenty of sleep is needed in order to lose weight effectively. Without the right amount of sleep, your body will feel stressed, and this could result in your metabolism slowing down. It might cause it to store fat instead of burning fat. When you feel tired, you are more tempted to drink more lattes for energy, eat a snack to give you an extra boost, or order takeout rather than cooking a healthy meal. Try to get between seven and nine hours of sleep each night. Understand that your body uses that time to burn fat without you even lifting a finger.

## Low on Electrolytes

Most people will experience the Keto flu when you begin this diet. This happens for two reasons: when your body changes from burning carbs to burning fat, your brain might not have enough energy, and this, in turn, can cause grogginess, headaches, and nausea. You could be dehydrated, and your electrolytes might be low since the Keto diet causes you to urinate often.

Getting the Keto flu is a great sign that you are heading in the right direction. You can lessen these symptoms by drinking more water or taking supplements that will balance your electrolytes.

## Consuming Hidden Carbs

Many foods look like they are low carb, but they aren't. You can find carbs in salad dressings, sauces, and condiments. Be sure to check nutrition labels before you try new foods to make sure it doesn't have any hidden sugar or carbs. It just takes a few seconds to skim the label, and it might be the difference between whether or not you'll lose weight.

If you have successfully ruled out all of the above, but you still aren't losing weight, you might need to talk with your doctor to make sure you don't have any health problems that could be preventing your weight loss. This can be frustrating, but stick with it, stay positive, and stay in the game. When the Keto diet is done correctly, it is one of the best ways to lose weight.

# 6. CHALLENGES SENIORS OVER 50 FACE DURING KETO DIET AND HOW TO AVOID THEM

The Keto diet is quite simple, just eat 75% fats, 20% protein and 5% carbs. It is a general practice most ketogenic beginners follow, and they maintain their body quite quickly. However, when you cross the age of 50, there are many challenges which you have to go through. Below is the list of those challenges along with their solutions.

## Keto-Flu

An abrupt shift of diet, from the normal intake of carbs to a limited amount, can cause Keto-flu, also known as carb withdrawal. It usually occurs after one to two days of withdrawal. Its symptoms include headache, muscle soreness, poor focus, sugar cravings, brain fog, irritability, insomnia, or weakness. Your body will take some time to switch from burning carbohydrates to burning fats. Therefore, an abrupt transformation of diet sends your body into starvation mode, hence giving you those unpleasant symptoms. Follow the below tips to help you ease discomforts and symptoms of Keto flu.

## Stay Well Hydrated

How much you should drink depends on your body weight. Divide your body weight by 2. The resulting number of ounces is the water you need to drink per day. The best way to add water is by consuming bone broth in your diet. It will provide not only electrolytes such as potassium and sodium to your body but also water.

## Electrolytes Supplementation

Electrolytes such as sodium, magnesium and potassium are the key players when it comes to getting better and faster results on a Keto diet. If that is not enough in your body, which is usually common if you are on a low carb diet, try incorporating them by taking electrolytes supplements.

## Consume More Healthy Fats

To enhance your adaptation phase, try to eat a lot of high-quality fat such as MCT oils because it travels straight to the liver after digestion as compared to other fats; hence it can be used immediately.

## Consume Exogenous Ketone Supplement

Exogenous ketone supplements aid fatigue and elevate energy levels by increasing the ketone levels in the blood. If you opt for this path, go for a smaller dose of these supplements. Take them, especially during the first five days of the Keto flu.

## Muscle Cramps and Dehydration

Carbs need water for their storage, unlike fats. Hence, instead of being retained, a smaller amount of water is stored during the Keto diet, and more amount of sodium is excreted by the kidneys. Due to this, you can easily get dehydrated while on the Keto diet, especially at the beginning. Due to this condition, low electrolyte concentration and dehydration, muscle cramping is certain.

## Solution

- Consult your doctor and complain to him/her about the problems you are facing.

- Add electrolytes supplements, as tackled under Keto flu, especially the three major electrolytes such as potassium, sodium and magnesium.

- Ensure drinking a lot of water in order to remain hydrated; remember the rule of dividing your body weight by 2.

## Insomnia

Although, there is not any research that has shown the effect of a Keto diet on sleep deprivation, there some people who have complained about lack of quality sleep during the Keto diet. If this is the case with you, then once in a while eating some high-quality carbs before bed can prove to be of huge help.

## Solution

Before sleeping, take one teaspoon of raw honey. This will give your body adequate high-quality carbs during your sleep.

## Brain Fog

When you eat fewer carbs, your body demands it; "I am hungry, and I want something to eat." When its wish isn't accommodated, it makes you fuzzy-headed. This is the brain's way of demanding more glucose. Because, up until now, that's the only fuel it has ever known.

## Solution

The best solution to remedy this condition is to ignore it and keep eating fat simply! Ultimately, your brain will adapt to its new fuel, and your head will become clearer than ever before.

## Constipation

Consuming carbs lesser than 20g of per day means insufficient fibers, which ultimately results in constipation and irritable bowel syndrome. Constipation also occurs when you are not drinking enough water. Following are some remedies to aid you in your constipation.

## Solution

- Add leafy and good vegetables to your diet.

- Try cyclical Keto from time to time. This will enable you to eat foods like butternut squash and sweet potatoes.

- Add enough natural salt such as Himalayan pink salt to your diet to help you retain water and make your bowels regular.

- Always remain hydrated and take electrolytes supplements.

- Do exercise regularly, it will also help you in relieving constipation problems.

- Try to take the recommended dosage of a good-quality digestive enzyme before or after every meal.

- Consume psyllium husk every morning. Mix 1 teaspoon in ½ cup of water and let it sit for 1 minute before drinking.

## Diarrhea

Some people have diarrhea difficulties while on the Keto diet. Your body may react this way because of an increasing amount of fat intake; as it isn't yet able to produce and store enough bile to break down all the fat, you're eating.

## Solution

- Reduce the amount of fat you're eating by at least 10 percent.

- Simultaneously, increase the number of fermented foods in your diets such as kombucha, water kefir, sauerkraut, kimchi, or your favorite fermented vegetable.

- Add apple cider vinegar to your drinks and salad dressings.

- Consider trying an ox bile supplement.

- To cure diarrhea, lower your fat intake for seven days—or until you are adapted to the new changes. Then, gradually increase your fat intake back up to where it was.

## Keto Rash

Keto rash also called prurigo pigmentosa is an itchy red rash that can develop on neck, chest, back and armpit areas; it is neither dangerous nor life-threatening. Although very rare, it sometimes occurs when people follow a strict ketogenic diet, usually 80 percent fat or higher. Other causative agents are hormonal imbalances, allergens exposure and gut bacteria.

**Solution**

- Support your skin with adequate supplements and anti-inflammatory foods such as DHA, omega-3 supplements, or turmeric latte. This will boost the healing time while soothing the rash.

- Keep yourself away from irritants like heat, sweat, or friction. Keto rash just like other rashes that can become worse when connecting with irritants. Avoid these irritants by putting on loose and breathable clothes, avoiding scented products or perfumes or any sweat-stimulating exercise until your skin is properly healed.

- Reintroduce some carbs in your diet, though avoid consuming a lot of bread. However, if rash occurs after a sudden shift to a Keto lifestyle, it is essential for you to bring back some high quality and healthy carbs such as butternut squash, pumpkin, carrots, yams and sweet potatoes.

# 7. FOODS ALLOWED IN THE KETO DIET

To make the most of your diet, there are prohibited foods, and others that are allowed, but in limited quantities. Here are the foods allowed in the ketogenic diet:

## Food Allowed in Unlimited Quantities

### Lean or Fatty Meats

No matter which meat you choose, it contains no carbohydrates so that you can have fun! Pay attention to the quality of your meat, and the amount of fat. Alternate between fatty meats and lean meats!

Here are some examples of lean meats:

- Beef: sirloin steak, roast beef, 5% minced steak, roast, flank steak, tenderloin, grisons meat, tripe, kidneys

- Horse: roti, steak

- Pork: tenderloin, bacon, kidneys

- Veal: cutlet, shank, tenderloin, sweetbread, liver

- Chicken and turkey: cutlet, skinless thigh, ham

- Rabbit

Here are some examples of fatty meats:

- Lamb: leg, ribs, brain

- Beef: minced steak 10, 15, 20%, ribs, rib steak, tongue, marrow

- Pork: ribs, brain, dry ham, black pudding, white pudding, bacon, terrine, rillettes, salami, sausage, sausages, and merguez

- Veal: roast, paupiette, marrow, brain, tongue, dumplings

- Chicken and turkey: thigh with skin

- Guinea fowl

- Capon

- Turkey

- Goose: foie gras

**Lean or Fatty Fish**

The fish does not contain carbohydrates so that you can consume unlimited! As with meat, there are lean fish and fatty fish, pay attention to the amount of fat you eat and remember to vary your intake of fish. Oily fish have the advantage of containing a lot of good cholesterol, so it is beneficial for protection against cardiovascular disease! It will be advisable to consume fatty fish more than lean fish, to be able to manage your protein intake: if you consume lean fish, you will have a significant protein intake and little lipids, whereas with fatty fish, you will have a balanced protein and fat intake!

Here are some examples of lean fish:

- Cod

- Colin

- Seabream

- Whiting

- Sole

- Turbot

- Limor career

- Location

- Pike

- Ray

Here are some examples of oily fish:

- Swordfish

- Salmon

- Tuna

- Trout

- Monkfish

- Herring

- Mackerel

- Cod

- Sardine

## Eggs

The eggs contain no carbohydrates, so you can consume as much as you want. It is often said that eggs are full of cholesterol and that you have to limit their intake, but the more cholesterol you eat, the less your body will produce by itself! In addition, it's not just poor-quality cholesterol so that you can consume 6 per week without risk! And if you want to eat more but you are afraid of your cholesterol and I have not convinced you, remove the yellow!

## Vegetables and Raw Vegetables

Yes, you can eat vegetables. But you have to be careful which ones: you can eat leafy vegetables (salad, spinach, kale, red cabbage, Chinese cabbage...) and flower vegetables (cauliflower, broccoli, Romanesco cabbage...) as well as avocado, cucumbers, zucchini or leeks, which do not contain many carbohydrates.

## The Oils

It's oil, so it's only fat, so it's unlimited to eat, but choose your oil wisely! Prefer olive oil, rapeseed, nuts, sunflower or sesame for example!

## Foods Authorized in Moderate Quantities

## The Cold Cuts

As you know, there is bad cholesterol in cold meats, so you will need to moderate your intake: eat it occasionally!

## Fresh Cheeses and Plain Yogurts

Consume with moderation because they contain carbohydrates.

## Nuts and Oilseeds

They have low levels of carbohydrates, but are rich in saturated fatty acids, that's why they should moderate their consumption. Choose almonds, hazelnuts, Brazil nuts or pecans.

## Coconut (in Oil, Cream or Milk)

It contains saturated fatty acids, that's why we limit its consumption. Cream and coconut oil contain a lot of medium-chain triglycerides (MCTs), which increase the level of ketones, essential to stay in ketosis.

## Berries and Red Fruits

They contain carbohydrates, in reasonable quantities, but you should not abuse them to avoid ketosis (blueberries, blackberries, raspberries...).

# 8. KETO GROCERY LIST

I've had people complain about the difficulty of switching their grocery list to one that's Ketogenic-friendly. The fact is that food is expensive—and most of the food you have in your fridge is probably packed full of carbohydrates. This is why if you're committing to a Ketogenic Diet, you need to do a clean sweep. That's right—everything that's packed with carbohydrates should be identified and set aside to make sure you're not eating more than you should. You can donate them to a charity before going out and buying your new Keto-friendly shopping list.

## Seafood

Seafood means fish like sardines, mackerel, and wild salmon. It's also a good idea to add some shrimp, tuna, mussels, and crab into your diet. This is going to be a tad expensive but definitely worth it in the long run. What's the common denominator in all these food items? The secret is omega-3 fatty acids which are credited for lots of health benefits. You want to add food rich in omega-3 fatty acids to your diet.

## Low-Carb Vegetables

Not all vegetables are good for you when it comes to the Ketogenic Diet. The vegetable choices should be limited to those with low carbohydrate counts. Pack up your cart with items like spinach, eggplant, arugula, broccoli, and cauliflower. You can also put in bell peppers, cabbage, celery, kale, Brussels sprouts, mushrooms, zucchini, and fennel.

So what's in them? Well, aside from the fact that they're low-carb, these vegetables also contain loads of fiber which makes digestion easier. Of course, there's also the presence of vitamins, minerals, antioxidants, and various other nutrients that you need for day to day life. Which ones should you avoid? Steer clear of the starch-packed vegetables like carrots, turnips, and beets. As a rule, you go for the vegetables that are green and leafy.

## Fruits Low in Sugar

During an episode of sugar-craving, it's usually a good idea to pick low-sugar fruit items. Believe it or not, there are lots of those in the market! Just make sure to stock up on any of these: avocado, blackberries, raspberries, strawberries, blueberries, lime, lemon, and coconut. Also, note that tomatoes are fruits too so feel free to make side dishes or dips with loads of tomatoes! Keep in mind that these fruits should be eaten fresh and not out of a can. If you do eat them fresh off the can, however, take a good look at the nutritional information at the back of the packaging. Avocadoes are particularly popular for those practicing the Ketogenic Diet because they contain LOTS of good kind of fat.

## Meat and Eggs

While some diets will tell you to skip the meat, the Ketogenic Diet actually encourages its consumption. Meat is packed with protein that will feed your muscles and give you a consistent source of energy throughout the day. It's a slow but sure burn when you eat protein as opposed to carbohydrates which are burned faster and therefore stored faster if you don't use them immediately.

But what kind of meat should you be eating? There's chicken, beef, pork, venison, turkey, and lamb. Keep in mind that quality plays a huge role here—you should be eating grass-fed organic beef or organic poultry if you want to make the most out of this food variety. The organic option lets you limit the possibility of ingesting toxins in your body due to the production process of these products. Plus, the preservation process also means there is added salt or sugar in the meat, which can throw off the whole diet.

## Nuts and Seeds

Nuts and seeds you should definitely add to your cart include: chia seeds, Brazil nuts, macadamia nuts, flaxseed, walnuts, hemp seeds, pecans, sesame seeds, almonds, hazelnut, and pumpkin seeds. They also contain lots of protein and very little sugar so they're great if you have the munchies. They're the ideal snack because they're quick, easy, and will keep you full. They're high in calories though, which is why lots of people steer clear of them. As I mentioned earlier though—the Ketogenic Diet has nothing to do with calories and everything to do with the nutrient you're eating. So don't pay too much attention to the calorie count and just remember that they're a good source of fats and protein.

## Dairy Products

OK—some people in their 50s already have a hard time processing dairy products, but for those who don't—you can happily add many of these to your diet. Make sure to consume sufficient amounts of cheese, plain Greek yogurt, cream butter, and cottage cheese. These dairy products are packed with calcium, protein, and the healthy kind of fat.

## Oils

Nope, we're not talking about essentials oils but rather, MCT oil, coconut oil, avocado oil, nut oils, and even extra-virgin olive oil. You can start using those for your frying needs to create healthier food options. The beauty of these oils is that they add flavor to the food, making sure you don't get bored quickly with the recipes. Try picking up different types of Keto-friendly oils to add some variety to your cooking.

## Coffee and Tea

The good news is that you don't have to skip coffee if you're going on a Ketogenic Diet. The bad news is that you can't go to Starbucks anymore and order their blended coffee choices. Instead, beverages would be limited to unsweetened tea or unsweetened coffee in order to keep the sugar consumption low. Opt for organic coffee and tea products to make the most out of these powerful antioxidants.

## Dark Chocolate

Yes—chocolate is still on the menu, but it is limited to just dark chocolate. Technically, this means eating chocolate that is 70 percent cacao, which would make the taste a bit bitter.

## Sugar Substitutes

Later in the recipes part of this book, you might be surprised at some of the ingredients required in the list. This is because while sweeteners are an important part of food preparation, you can't just use any kind of sugar in your recipe. Remember: the typical sugar is pure carbohydrate. Even if you're not eating carbohydrates, if you're dumping lots of sugar in your food—you're not really following the Ketogenic Diet principles.

So what do you do? You find sugar substitutes. The good news is that there are LOTS of those in the market. You can get rid of the old sugar and use any of these as a good substitute.

- Stevia. This is perhaps the most familiar one on this list. It's a natural sweetener derived from plants and contains very few calories. Unlike your typical sugar, stevia may actually help lower the sugar levels instead of causing it to spike. Note though that it's sweeter than actual sugar so when cooking with stevia, you'll need to lower the amount used. Typically, the ratio is 200grams of sugar per 1 teaspoon of powdered stevia.

- Sucralose. It contains zero calories and zero carbohydrates. It's actually an artificial sweetener and does not metabolize—hence the complete lack of carbohydrates. Splenda is actually a sweetener derived from sucralose. Note though that you don't want to use this as a baking substitute for sugar. Its best use is for coffee, yogurt, and oatmeal sweetening. Note though that like stevia, it's also very sweet—in fact, it's actually 600 times sweeter than the typical sugar. Use sparingly.

- Erythritol. It's a naturally occurring compound that interacts with the tongue's sweet taste receptors. Hence, it mimics the taste of sugar without actually being sugar. It does contain calories, but only about 5% of the calories you'll find in the typical sugar. Note though that it doesn't dissolve very well so anything prepared with this sweetener will have a gritty feeling. This can be problematic if you're using the product for baking. As for sweetness, the typical ratio is 1 1/3 cup for 1 cup of sugar.

- Xylitol. Like erythritol, xylitol is a type of sugar alcohol that's commonly used in sugar-free gum. While it still contains calories, the calories are just 3 per gram. It's a sweetener that's good for diabetic patients because it doesn't raise the sugar levels or insulin in the body. The great thing about this is that you don't have to do any computations when using it for baking, cooking, or fixing a drink. The ratio of it with sugar is 1 to 1 so you can quickly make the substitution in the recipe.

### What About Condiments?

Condiments are still on the table, but they won't be as tasty as you're used to. Your options include mustard, olive oil mayonnaise, oil-based salad dressings, and unsweetened ketchup. Of all these condiments, ketchup is the one with the most sugar, so make a point of looking for one with reduced sugar content. Or maybe avoid ketchup altogether and stick to mustard?

### What About Snacks?

The good news is that there are packed snacks for those who don't have the time to make it themselves. Sugarless nut butters, dried seaweeds, nuts, and sugar-free jerky are all available in stores. The nuts and seeds discussed in a previous paragraph all make for excellent snack options.

### What About Labels?

Let's not fool ourselves into thinking that we can cook food every single day. The fact is that there will be days when there will be purchases for the sake of convenience. There are also instances when you'll have problems finding the right ingredients for a given recipe. Hence, you'll need to find substitutes for certain ingredients without losing the "Keto-friendly" vibe of the product.

So what should be done? Well, you need to learn how to read labels. Food doesn't have to be specially made to be keto-friendly, you just have to make sure that it doesn't contain any of the unfriendly nutrients or that the carbohydrate content is low enough.

# 9. BREAKFAST

 **PREPARATION: 5 MIN**

 **COOKING: 5 MIN**

 **SERVES: 4**

# 1. ALMOND FLOUR PANCAKES

## INGREDIENTS

- ½ cup almond flour
- ½ cup cream cheese
- 4 medium eggs
- ½ tsp cinnamon
- ½ tsp granulated sweetener
- 1 tsp grass-fed butter
- 1 tbsp sugar-free syrup

## DIRECTIONS

1. Add all the ingredients into a blender and let them blend in well. Once done, set the batter aside.
2. On a non-stick pan at medium heat, fry pancakes with melted butter. Once the center starts to bubble, turn over. Once done with the pancake, move on to the rest, using the batter.
3. Finally, serve your pancakes warm, along with some low carb fruit or with an exquisite side of sugar-free syrup to enjoy a healthy and tasty breakfast.

## NUTRITION

- Calories: 234
- Fat: 20g
- Carbohydrates: 4g
- Fiber: 1.5g
- Net carbs: 2.5g
- Protein: 11g

**PREPARATION: 20 MIN**

**COOKING: 40 MIN**

**SERVES: 2**

# 2. AVOCADO TOAST

## INGREDIENTS

- ½ cup grass-fed butter
- 2 tbsp coconut oil
- 7 large eggs
- 1 tsp baking powder
- 2 cups almond flour
- ½ tsp xanthan gum
- ½ tsp kosher salt
- 1 medium avocado

## DIRECTIONS

1. Preheat over at 350°F. Beat eggs for around two minutes with a mixer at high speed. Then, add coconut oil and butter (both melted) to the eggs and continue beating. Ensure that oil and butter are not too warm to cook the eggs. Add remaining bread ingredients and mix well. Now, the batter should become thick. Pour batter in a non-stick loaf pan lined with parchment paper. Let it bake for 45 minutes or until the fork comes clean through the middle.
2. For topping, toast two slices of your keto bread to your liking. Slice the whole avocado thinly, without the skin or pit. Use these to make one long strip of overlapping slices. Roll these into a spiral and that is it! Enjoy your keto bread with avocado topping.

## NUTRITION

- Calories: 350
- Fat: 32g
- Carbohydrates: 7g
- Fiber: 4g
- Net carbs: 3g
- Protein: 10g

**PREPARATION: 10 MIN**

**COOKING: 10 MIN**

**SERVES: 4**

# 3. CHICKEN AVOCADO EGG BACON SALAD

## INGREDIENTS

- 12 oz. cooked chicken breast
- 6 slices crumbled bacon
- 3 boiled eggs cut into cubes
- 1 cup cherry tomatoes cut into halves
- 1/2 small sliced red onion
- 1 large avocado(s)
- 1/2 stick finely chopped celery
- Salad Dressing
- 1/2 cup olive oil mayonnaise
- 2 tbsp. sour cream
- 1 tsp Dijon mustard
- 4 tbsp. extra virgin olive oil
- 2 cloves minced garlic
- 2 tsp lemon juice
- 4 cups lettuce
- Salt and pepper to taste

## DIRECTIONS

1. Combine all the ingredients together and mix them well for the salad dressing. Then, combine chicken, tomatoes, bacon, eggs, red onions, and celery together. Add about ¾ of the salad dressing and mix them well. Add the avocado and toss together gently. Check the taste and, if needed, add the remainder of the salad dressing as well. Finally, add salt and pepper to taste and then serve it over lettuce.

## NUTRITION

- Calories: 387
- Fat: 27g
- Carbohydrates: 2.5g

- Fiber: 1g
- Net carbs: 1.5g
- Protein: 24g

**PREPARATION: 10 MIN**

**COOKING: 45 MIN**

**SERVES: 4**

# 4. BACON WRAPPED CHICKEN BREAST

## INGREDIENTS

- 4 boneless, skinless chicken breast
- 8 oz. sharp cheddar cheese
- 8 slices bacon
- 4 oz. sliced jalapeno peppers
- 1 tsp garlic powder
- Salt and pepper to taste

## DIRECTIONS

1. Preheat the oven at around 350°F. Ensure to season both sides of chicken breast well with salt, garlic powder, and pepper. Place the chicken breast on a non-stick baking sheet (foil-covered). Cover the chicken with cheese and add jalapeno slices. Cut the bacon slices in half and then place the four halves over each piece of chicken. Bake for around 30 to 45 minutes at most. If the chicken is set but the bacon still feels undercooked, you may want to put it under the broiler for a few minutes. Once done, serve hot with a side of low carb garlic parmesan roasted asparagus.

## NUTRITION

- Calories: 640
- Fat: 48g
- Carbohydrates: 6g

- Fiber: 3g
- Net carbs: 3g
- Protein: 47g

**PREPARATION: 15 MIN**

**COOKING: 10 MIN**

**SERVES: 4**

# 5. EGG SALAD

## INGREDIENTS

- 6 eggs
- 2 tbsp mayonnaise
- 1 tsp Dijon mustard
- 1 tsp lemon juice
- Salt and pepper to taste
- Lettuce leaves

## DIRECTIONS

1. In a medium saucepan, place the solid eggs gently.
2. Add some cold water so that the eggs are covered around an inch. Boil them for around 10 minutes.
3. Once done, remove them from the heat and let them cool. Peel the eggs while running them under cold water. Now add these in a food processor and pulse until they are chopped.
4. Add and stir mayonnaise, lemon juice, mustard, and salt and pepper. Ensure to taste and then adjust as necessary.
5. Finally, serve them with a bit of lettuce leaves and, if needed, bacon for wrapping.

## NUTRITION

- Calories: 222
- Fat: 19g
- Net carbs: 1g

- Protein: 13g

**PREPARATION: 10 MIN**

**COOKING: 30 MIN**

**SERVES: 12**

# 6. BLUEBERRY MUFFINS

## INGREDIENTS

- 1 container Greek yogurt
- 3 large eggs
- 1/2 tsp vanilla extract
- 1/4 tsp salt
- 2 1/2 cups almond flour
- 1/4 cup Swerve sweetener (add more if using plain Greek yogurt)
- 2 tsp baking powder
- Water if needed to thin
- 1/2 cup fresh blueberries

## DIRECTIONS

1. Preheat oven at 325°F. Simultaneously, line-up a clean muffin pan with around 12 parchment liners. Combine yogurt, vanilla, eggs, and salt in a blender. Blend the mixture till it is smooth. Add almond flour, baking powder and sweetener. Now, blend again until it is smooth. If the batter is thick, add one tablespoon of water at a time. The batter should be thick, but it must be pourable.
2. Add in blueberries and divide these equally for the prepared muffin cups. Finally, bake these for 25 to 30 minutes. Use a tester and insert it right in the middle. If it comes out clean, your muffins are ready.

## NUTRITION

- Calories: 163
- Net carbs: 3.8g
- Fat: 12.9g
- Protein: 7.6g

**PREPARATION: 5 MIN**

**COOKING: 10 MIN**

**SERVES: 2**

# 7. BACON HASH

## INGREDIENTS

- 1 Small green pepper
- 2 Jalapenos
- 1 Small onion
- 4 Eggs
- 6 Bacon slices

## DIRECTIONS

1. Chop the bacon into chunks using a food processor. Set aside for now. Slice the onions and peppers into thin strips. Dice the jalapenos as small as possible.
2. Heat a skillet and fry the veggies. Once browned, combine the fixings and cook until crispy. Place on a serving dish with the eggs.

## NUTRITION

- Carbohydrates: 9grams
- Protein: 23grams
- Fats: 24grams

- Calories: 366

# 8. BAGELS WITH CHEESE

## INGREDIENTS

- 2 ½ cups Mozzarella cheese
- 1 tsp. Baking powder
- 3 oz. Cream cheese
- 1 ½ Almond flour
- 2 Eggs

## DIRECTIONS

1. Shred the mozzarella and combine with the flour, baking powder, and cream cheese in a mixing container. Pop into the microwave for about one minute. Mix well.
2. Let the mixture cool and add the eggs. Break apart into six sections and shape into round bagels. Note: You can also sprinkle with a seasoning of your choice or pinch of salt if desired.
3. Bake them for approximately 12 to 15 minutes. Serve or cool and store.

## NUTRITION

- Carbohydrates: 8grams
- Protein: 19grams
- Fats: 31grams

- Calories: 374

**PREPARATION: 10 MIN**

**COOKING: 15 MIN**

**SERVES: 2**

# 9. CAULI FLITTERS

## INGREDIENTS

- 2 eggs
- 1 head of cauliflower
- 1 tbsp. yeast
- Sea salt, black pepper
- 1-2 tbsp. ghee
- 1 tbsp. turmeric
- 2/3 cup almond flour

## DIRECTIONS

1. Place the cauliflower into a large pot and start to boil it for 8 mins. Add the florets into a food processor and pulse them.
2. Add the eggs, almond flour, yeast, turmeric, salt and pepper to a mixing bowl. Stir well. Form into patties.
3. Heat your ghee to medium in a skillet. Form your fritters and cook until golden on each side (3-4 mins).
4. Serve it while hot.

## NUTRITION

- Calories: 238 kcal
- Fat: 23g
- Carbs: 5g

- Protein: 6g

**PREPARATION: 2 MIN**

**COOKING: 8 MIN**

**SERVES: 4**

# 10. SCRAMBLED EGGS

## INGREDIENTS

- 4 oz. butter
- 8 eggs
- Salt and pepper for taste

## DIRECTIONS

1. Crack the eggs in a bowl, and whisk them together, while seasoning it.
2. Melt the butter in a skillet over medium heat, but don't turn it into brown.
3. Pour the eggs into the skillet and cook it for 1-2 mins, until they look and feel fluffy and creamy.
4. Tip: If you want to shake things up, you can pair this one up with bacon, salmon, or maybe avocado as well.

## NUTRITION

- Carbs: 1g
- Fat: 31g
- Protein: 11g
- Calories: 327 kcal

**PREPARATION: 5 MIN**

**COOKING: 30 MIN**

**SERVES: 4**

# 11. FRITTATA WITH SPINACH

## INGREDIENTS

- 8 eggs
- 8 ozs. fresh spinach
- 5 ozs. diced bacon
- 5 ozs. shredded cheese
- 1 cup heavy whipping cream
- 2 tbsps. butter
- salt and pepper

## DIRECTIONS

1. Preheat the oven to 350°F
2. Fry the bacon until crispy, add the spinach and cook until wilted. Set them aside.
3. Whisk the cream and eggs together, and pour it into the baking dish.
4. Add the cheese, spinach, and bacon on the top, and place in the oven. Bake for 25-30 minutes, until golden brown on top.

## NUTRITION

- Carbs: 4g
- Fat: 59g
- Protein: 27g

- Calories: 661 kcal

**PREPARATION: 5 MIN**

**COOKING: 10 MIN**

**SERVES: 2**

# 12. CHEESE OMELET

## INGREDIENTS

- 6 eggs
- 3 ozs. ghee
- 7 ozs. shredded cheddar cheese
- Salt and pepper

## DIRECTIONS

1. Whisk the eggs until smooth. Compound half of the cheese and season it with salt and pepper.
2. Melt the butter in a pan. Pour in the mixture and let it sit for a few minutes (3-4)
3. When the mixture is looking good, add the other half of the cheese. Serve immediately.

## NUTRITION

- Carbs: 4g
- Fat: 80g
- Protein: 40g

- Calories: 897 kcal

**PREPARATION: 5 MIN**

**COOKING: 15 MIN**

**SERVES: 4**

# 13. CAPICOLA EGG CUPS

## INGREDIENTS

- 8 eggs
- 1 cup cheddar cheese
- 4 oz. capicola or bacon (slices)
- Salt, pepper, basil

## DIRECTIONS

1. Preheat the oven to 400°F. You will need 8 wells of a standard-size muffin pan.
2. Place the slices in the 8 wells, forming a cup shape. Sprinkle into each cup some of the cheese, according to your liking.
3. Crack an egg into each cup, season them with salt and pepper.
4. Bake for 10-15 mins. Serve hot, top it with basil.

## NUTRITION

- Carbs: 1g
- Fat: 11g
- Protein: 16g

- Calories: 171kcal

**PREPARATION: 5 MINUTES PLUS OVERNIGHT TO CHILL**

**COOKING: 10 MIN**

**SERVES: 1**

# 14. OVERNIGHT "NOATS"

## INGREDIENTS

- 2 tablespoons hulled hemp seeds
- 1 tablespoon chia seeds
- ½ scoop (about 8grams) collagen powder
- ½ cup unsweetened nut or seed milk (hemp, almond, coconut, and cashew)

## DIRECTIONS

1. In a small mason jar or glass container, combine the hemp seeds, chia seeds, collagen, and milk.
2. Secure tightly with a lid, shake well, and refrigerate overnight.

## NUTRITION

- Calories: 263
- Total Fat: 19g
- Protein: 16g

- Total Carbs: 7g
- Fiber: 5g
- Net Carbs: 2g

**PREPARATION: 5 MIN**

**COOKING: 20 MIN**

**SERVES: 1**

# 15. FROZEN KETO COFFEE

## INGREDIENTS

- 12 ounces coffee, chilled
- 1 scoop MCT powder (or 1 tablespoon MCT oil)
- 1 tablespoon heavy (whipping) cream
- Pinch ground cinnamon
- Dash sweetener (optional)
- ½ cup ice

## DIRECTIONS

1. In a blender, combine the coffee, MCT powder, cream, cinnamon, sweetener (if using), and ice. Blend until smooth.

## NUTRITION

- Calories: 127
- Total Fat: 13g
- Protein: 1g

- Total Carbs: 1.5g
- Fiber: 1g
- Net Carbs: 0.5g

**PREPARATION: 5 MIN**

**COOKING: 5 MIN**

**SERVES: 8**

# 16. EASY SKILLET PANCAKES

## INGREDIENTS

- 8 ounces cream cheese
- 8 eggs
- 2 tablespoons coconut flour
- 2 teaspoons baking powder
- 1 teaspoon ground cinnamon
- ½ teaspoon vanilla extract
- 1 teaspoon liquid stevia or sweetener of choice (optional)
- 2 tablespoons butter

## DIRECTIONS

1. In a blender, combine the cream cheese, eggs, coconut flour, baking powder, cinnamon, vanilla, and stevia (if using). Blend until smooth.
2. In a large skillet over medium heat, melt the butter.
3. Use half the mixture to pour four evenly sized pancakes and cook for about a minute, until you see bubbles on top. Flip the pancakes and cook for another minute. Remove from the pan and add more butter or oil to the skillet if needed. Repeat with the remaining batter.
4. Top with butter and eat right away, or freeze the pancakes in a freezer-safe resealable bag with sheets of parchment in between, for up to 1 month.

## NUTRITION

- Calories: 179
- Total Fat: 15g
- Protein: 8g
- Total Carbs: 3g
- Fiber: 1g
- Net Carbs: 2g

# 17. QUICK KETO BLENDER MUFFINS

## INGREDIENTS

- Butter, ghee, or coconut oil for greasing the pan
- 6 eggs
- 8 ounces cream cheese, at room temperature
- 2 scoops flavored collagen powder
- 1 teaspoon ground cinnamon
- 1 teaspoon baking powder
- Few drops or dash sweetener (optional)

## DIRECTIONS

1. Preheat the oven to 350°F. Grease a 12-cup muffin pan very well with butter, ghee, or coconut oil. Alternatively, you can use silicone cups or paper muffin liners.
2. In a blender, combine the eggs, cream cheese, collagen powder, cinnamon, baking powder, and sweetener (if using). Blend until well combined and pour the mixture into the muffin cups, dividing equally.
3. Bake for 22 to 25 minutes until the muffins are golden brown on top and firm.
4. Let cool then store in a glass container or plastic bag in the refrigerator for up to 2 weeks or in the freezer for up to 3 months.
5. To serve refrigerated muffins, heat in the microwave for 30 seconds. To serve from frozen, thaw in the refrigerator overnight and then microwave for 30 seconds, or microwave straight from the freezer for 45 to 60 seconds or until heated through.

## NUTRITION

- Calories: 120
- Total Fat: 10g
- Protein: 6g

- Total Carbs: 1.5g
- Fiber: 0g
- Net Carbs: 1.5g

**PREPARATION: 10 MIN**

**COOKING: 15 MIN**

**SERVES: 8**

# 18. KETO EVERYTHING BAGELS

## INGREDIENTS

- 2 cups shredded mozzarella cheese
- 2 tablespoons labneh cheese (or cream cheese)
- 1½ cups almond flour
- 1 egg
- 2 teaspoons baking powder
- ¼ teaspoon sea salt

## DIRECTIONS

1. Preheat the oven to 400°F.
2. In a microwave-safe bowl, combine the mozzarella and labneh cheeses. Microwave for 30 seconds, stir, then microwave for another 30 seconds. Stir well. If not melted completely, microwave for another 10 to 20 seconds.
3. Add the almond flour, egg, baking powder, and salt to the bowl and mix well. Form into a dough using a spatula or your hands.
4. Cut the dough into 8 roughly equal pieces and form into balls.
5. Roll each dough ball into a cylinder, then pinch the ends together to seal.
6. Place the dough rings in a nonstick donut pan or arrange them on a parchment paper–lined baking sheet.
7. Sprinkle with the seasoning and bake for 12 to 15 minutes or until golden brown.
8. Store in plastic bags in the freezer and defrost overnight in the refrigerator. Reheat in the oven or toaster for a quick grab-and-go breakfast.

## NUTRITION

- Calories: 241
- Total Fat: 19g
- Protein: 12g

- Total Carbs: 5.5g
- Fiber: 2.5g
- Net Carbs: 3g

**PREPARATION: 20 MIN**

**COOKING: 15 MIN**

**SERVES: 4**

# 19. TURMERIC CHICKEN AND KALE SALAD WITH FOOD, LEMON AND HONEY

## INGREDIENTS

**For the chicken:**
- 1 teaspoon of clarified butter or 1 tablespoon of coconut oil
- ½ medium brown onion, diced
- 250-300g/9 ounces minced chicken meat or diced chicken legs
- 1 large garlic clove, diced
- 1 teaspoon of turmeric powder
- 1 teaspoon of lime zest
- ½ lime juice
- ½ teaspoon of salt + pepper

**For the salad:**
- 6 stalks of broccoli or 2 cups of broccoli flowers
- 2 tablespoons of pumpkin seeds (seeds)
- 3 large cabbage leaves, stems removed and chopped
- ½ sliced avocado
- Handful of fresh coriander leaves, chopped
- Handful of fresh parsley leaves, chopped

**For the dressing:**
- 3 tablespoons of lime juice
- 1 small garlic clove, diced or grated
- 3 tablespoons of virgin olive oil (I used 1 tablespoon of avocado oil and 2 tablespoons of EVO)
- 1 teaspoon of raw honey
- ½ teaspoon whole or Dijon mustard
- ½ teaspoon of sea salt with pepper

## DIRECTIONS

1. Heat the coconut oil in a pan. Add the onion and sauté over medium heat for 4-5 minutes, until golden brown. Add the minced chicken and garlic and stir 2-3 minutes over medium-high heat, separating.
2. Add your turmeric, lime zest, lime juice, salt and pepper, and cook, stirring consistently, for another 3-4 minutes. Set the ground beef aside.
3. While your chicken is cooking, put a small saucepan of water to the boil. Add your broccoli and cook for 2 minutes. Rinse with cold water and cut into 3-4 pieces each.
4. Add the pumpkin seeds to the chicken pan and toast over medium heat for 2 minutes, frequently stirring to avoid burning. Season with a little salt. Set aside. Raw pumpkin seeds are also good to use.
5. Put the chopped cabbage in a salad bowl and pour it over the dressing. Using your hands, mix, and massage the cabbage with the dressing. This will soften the cabbage, a bit like citrus juice with fish or beef Carpaccio: it "cooks" it a little.
6. Finally, mix the cooked chicken, broccoli, fresh herbs, pumpkin seeds, and avocado slices.

## NUTRITION

- Calories: 232
- Fat: 11g
- Fiber: 9g

- Carbs: 8g
- Protein: 14g

**PREPARATION: 15 MIN**

**COOKING: 15 MIN**

**SERVES: 2**

# 20. BUCKWHEAT SPAGHETTI WITH CHICKEN CABBAGE AND SAVORY FOOD RECIPES IN MASS SAUCE

## INGREDIENTS

**For the noodles:**
- 2-3 handfuls of cabbage leaves (removed from the stem and cut)
- Buckwheat noodles 150g/5oz (100% buckwheat, without wheat)
- 3-4 shiitake mushrooms, sliced
- 1 teaspoon of coconut oil or butter
- 1 brown onion, finely chopped
- 1 medium chicken breast, sliced or diced
- 1 long red pepper, thinly sliced (seeds in or out depending on how hot you like it)
- 2 large garlic cloves, diced
- 2-3 tablespoons of Tamari sauce (gluten-free soy sauce)

**For the miso dressing:**
- 1 tablespoon and a half of fresh organic miso
- 1 tablespoon of Tamari sauce
- 1 tablespoon of extra virgin olive oil
- 1 tablespoon of lemon or lime juice
- 1 teaspoon of sesame oil (optional)

## DIRECTIONS

1. Boil a medium saucepan of water. Add the black cabbage and cook 1 minute, until it is wilted. Remove and reserve, but reserve the water and return to boiling. Add your soba noodles and cook according to the directions on the package (usually about 5 minutes). Rinse with cold water and reserve.
2. In the meantime, fry the shiitake mushrooms in a little butter or coconut oil (about a teaspoon) for 2-3 minutes, until its color is lightly browned on each side. Sprinkle with sea salt and reserve.
3. In that same pan, heat more coconut oil or lard over medium-high heat. Fry the onion and chili for 2-3 minutes, and then add the chicken pieces. Cook 5 minutes on medium heat, stirring a few times, then add the garlic, tamari sauce, and a little water. Cook for another 2-3 minutes, stirring continuously until your chicken is cooked.
4. Finally, add the cabbage and soba noodles and stir the chicken to warm it.
5. Stir the miso sauce and sprinkle the noodles at the end of the cooking, in this way you will keep alive all the beneficial probiotics in the miso.

## NUTRITION

- Calories: 305
- Fat: 11g
- Fiber: 7g
- Carbs: 9g
- Protein: 12g

**PREPARATION: 15 MIN**

**COOKING: 10 MIN**

**SERVES: 4**

# 21. ASIAN KING JUMPED JAMP

## INGREDIENTS

- 150g/5 oz. of raw shelled prawns, not chopped
- Two teaspoons of tamari (you can use soy sauce if you don't avoid gluten)
- Two teaspoons of extra virgin olive oil
- 75g/2.6 oz. soba (buckwheat pasta)
- 1 garlic clove, finely chopped
- 1 bird's eye chili, finely chopped
- 1 teaspoon finely chopped fresh ginger.
- 20g/0.7 oz. of sliced red onions
- 40g/1.4 oz. of celery, cut and sliced
- 75g/2.6 oz. of chopped green beans
- 50g/1.7 oz. of chopped cabbage
- 100 ml/½ cup of chicken broth
- 5g celery or celery leaves

## DIRECTIONS

1. Heat a pan over high heat, and then cook the prawns in 1 teaspoon of tamari and 1 teaspoon of oil for 2-3 minutes. Transfer the prawns to a plate. Clean the pan with kitchen paper as it will be reused.
2. Cook your noodles in boiling water for 5-8 minutes or as indicated on the package. Drain and set aside.
3. Meanwhile, fry the garlic, chili and ginger, red onion, celery, beans, and cabbage in the remaining oil over medium-high heat for 2-3 minutes. Add your broth and allow it to boil, and then simmer for a minute or two, until the vegetables are cooked but crunchy.
4. Add shrimp, noodles and celery/celery leaves to the pan, bring to a boil again, then remove from the heat and serve.

## NUTRITION

- Calories: 223
- Protein: 34g
- Fat: 2g

- Carbs: 6g

# 22. BUCKWHEAT PASTA SALAD

## INGREDIENTS

- 50g/1.7 oz. buckwheat pasta
- Large handful of rockets
- A small handful of basil leaves
- Eight cherry tomatoes halved
- 1/2 avocado, diced
- Ten olives
- 1 tablespoon. extra olive virgin oil
- 20g/0.70 oz. pine nuts

## DIRECTIONS

1. Combine all the ingredients except your pine nuts. Arrange your combination on a plate, and then scatter the pine nuts over the top.

## NUTRITION

- Calories: 125
- Fat: 6g
- Fiber: 5g
- Carbs: 10g
- Protein: 11g

**PREPARATION: 35 MIN**

**COOKING: 0 MIN**

**SERVES: 2**

# 23. GREEK SALAD SKEWERS

## INGREDIENTS

- Two wooden skewers, soaked in water for 30 minutes before use
- Eight large black olives
- Eight cherry tomatoes
- 1 yellow pepper, cut into eight squares.
- ½ red onions, you can cut in half and separated into eight pieces
- 100g/3.5 oz. (about 10cm) cucumber, cut into four slices and halved
- 100g/3.5 oz. feta, cut into eight cubes

**For the dressing:**
- 1 tablespoon. extra olive virgin oil
- Juice of ½ lemons
- 1 teaspoon. of your balsamic vinegar
- ½ garlic clove, peeled and crushed
- Basil leaves chopped (or ½ teaspoon. dried mixed herbs to replace basil and oregano)
- Oregano leaves
- Salt and grounded black pepper

## DIRECTIONS

1. Blend each skewer with the salad ingredients in the order
2. Put all your dressing ingredients into a bowl and mix thoroughly. Pour over the skewers.

## NUTRITION

- Calories: 99
- Protein: 34g
- Fat: 4g

- Carbs: 5g

**PREPARATION: 20 MIN**

**COOKING: 40 MIN**

**SERVES: 3**

# 24. KALE, EDAMAME AND TOFU CURRY

## INGREDIENTS

- 1 tablespoon rapeseed oil
- 1 large onion, chopped
- 4 garlic cloves, peeled and grated
- 1 large thumb (7cm) fresh ginger, peeled and grated
- 1 red chili, deseeded and thinly sliced
- 1/2 teaspoon ground turmeric
- 1/4 teaspoon cayenne pepper
- 1 teaspoon paprika
- 1/2 teaspoon ground cumin
- 1 teaspoon salt
- 250g/9 oz. dried red lentils
- 1-liter boiling water
- 50g/1.7 oz. frozen soya beans
- 200g/7 oz. firm tofu, chopped into cubes
- 2 tomatoes, roughly chopped
- Juice of 1 lime
- 200g/7 oz. kale leaves stalk removed and torn

## DIRECTIONS

1. Put the oil in a pan over low heat. Add your onion and cook for 5 minutes before adding the garlic, ginger, and chili and cooking for a further 2 minutes. Add your turmeric, cayenne, paprika, cumin, and salt and Stir through before adding the red lentils and stirring again.
2. Pour in the boiling water and allow it to simmer for 10 minutes, reduce the heat and cook for about 20-30 minutes until the curry has a thick 'porridge' consistency.
3. Add your tomatoes, tofu and soya beans and cook for a further 5 minutes. Add your kale leaves and lime juice and cook until the kale is just tender.

## NUTRITION

- Calories: 133
- Carbohydrate: 54g
- Protein: 43g

**PREPARATION: MIN**

**COOKING: 45 MIN**

**SERVES: 4**

# 25. CHOCOLATE CUPCAKES WITH MATCHA ICING

## INGREDIENTS

- Toppings:
- 1/4 cup mixed berries for each cheesecake, frozen and thawed
- Filling ingredients:
- 1/2 teaspoon vanilla extract
- 1/2 teaspoon almond extract
- 3/4 cup sweetener
- 6 eggs
- 8 ounces cream cheese
- 16 ounces cottage cheese
- Crust ingredients:
- 4 tablespoons salted butter
- 2 tablespoons sweetener
- 2 cups almonds, whole

## DIRECTIONS

1. Preheat oven to 350°F.
2. Pulse almonds in a food processor, then add in butter and sweetener.
3. Pulse until all the ingredients mix well and a course dough is formed.
4. Coat twelve silicone muffin pans using foil or paper liners.
5. Divide the batter between the muffin pans, then press into the bottom part until it forms a crust and bake for about 8 minutes.
6. In the meantime, mix in a food processor the cream cheese and cottage cheese, then pulse until the mixture is smooth.
7. Put in the extracts and sweetener, then combine until well mixed.
8. Add in eggs and pulse again until it becomes smooth; you might need to scrape down the mixture from the sides of the processor. Share the batter between the muffin pans and then bake for around 30–40 minutes until the middle is not wobbly when you shake the muffin pan lightly.
9. Put aside until cooled completely, then put in the refrigerator for about 2 hours and then top with frozen and thawed berries.

## NUTRITION

- Fats: 12g
- Calories: 152
- Proteins: 6g

- Carbs: 3g

**PREPARATION: 20 MIN**

**COOKING: 0 MIN**

**SERVES: 4**

# 26. SESAME CHICKEN SALAD

## INGREDIENTS

- 1 tablespoon of sesame seeds
- 1 cucumber, peeled, halved lengthwise, without a teaspoon, and sliced.
- 100g/3.5 oz. cabbage, chopped
- 60g pak choi, finely chopped
- ½ red onion, thinly sliced
- Large parsley (20g/0.7 oz.), chopped.
- 150g/5 oz. cooked chicken, minced
- For the dressing:
- 1 tablespoon of extra virgin olive oil
- 1 teaspoon of sesame oil
- 1 lime juice
- 1 teaspoon of light honey
- 2 teaspoons soy sauce

## DIRECTIONS

1. Roast your sesame seeds in a dry pan for 2 minutes until they become slightly golden and fragrant.
2. Transfer to a plate to cool.
3. In a small bowl, mix olive oil, sesame oil, lime juice, honey, and soy sauce to prepare the dressing.
4. Place the cucumber, black cabbage, pak choi, red onion, and parsley in a large bowl and mix gently.
5. Pour over the dressing and mix again.
6. Distribute the salad between two dishes and complete with the shredded chicken. Sprinkle with sesame seeds just before serving.

## NUTRITION

- Calories: 345
- Fat: 5g
- Fiber: 2g
- Carbs: 10g
- Protein: 4g

**PREPARATION: 15 MIN**

**COOKING: 2 HOURS**

**SERVES: 6**

# 27. BACON APPETIZERS

## INGREDIENTS

- 1 pack Keto crackers
- ¾ cup Parmesan cheese, grated
- 1 lb. bacon, sliced thinly

## DIRECTIONS

1. Preheat your oven to 250 degrees F.
2. Arrange the crackers on a baking sheet.
3. Sprinkle cheese on top of each cracker.
4. Wrap each cracker with the bacon.
5. Bake in the oven for 2 hours.

## NUTRITION

- Calories: 440
- Total Fat: 33.4g
- Saturated Fat: 11g
- Cholesterol: 86mg
- Sodium: 1813mg
- Total Carbohydrate: 3.7g
- Dietary Fiber: 0.1g
- Total Sugars: 0.1g
- Protein: 29.4g
- Potassium: 432mg

**PREPARATION: 10 MIN**

**COOKING: 0 MIN**

**SERVES: 6**

# 28. ANTIPASTI SKEWERS

## INGREDIENTS

- 6 small mozzarella balls
- 1 tablespoon olive oil
- Salt to taste
- 1/8 teaspoon dried oregano
- 2 roasted yellow peppers, sliced into strips and rolled
- 6 cherry tomatoes
- 6 green olives, pitted
- 6 Kalamata olives, pitted
- 2 artichoke hearts, sliced into wedges
- 6 slices salami, rolled
- 6 leaves fresh basil

## DIRECTIONS

1. Toss the mozzarella balls in olive oil.
2. Season with salt and oregano.
3. Thread the mozzarella balls and the rest of the ingredients into skewers.
4. Serve in a platter.

## NUTRITION

- Calories: 180
- Total Fat: 11.8g
- Saturated Fat: 4.5g
- Cholesterol: 26mg
- Sodium: 482mg
- Total Carbohydrate: 11.7g
- Dietary Fiber: 4.8g
- Total Sugars: 4.1g
- Protein: 9.2g
- Potassium: 538mg

**PREPARATION: 30 MIN**

**COOKING: 60 MIN**

**SERVES: 10**

# 29. JALAPENO POPPERS

## INGREDIENTS

- 5 fresh jalapenos, sliced and seeded
- 4 oz. package cream cheese
- ¼ lb. bacon, sliced in half

## DIRECTIONS

1. Preheat your oven to 275 degrees F.
2. Place a wire rack over your baking sheet.
3. Stuff each jalapeno with cream cheese and wrap in bacon.
4. Secure with a toothpick.
5. Place on the baking sheet.
6. Bake for 1 hour and 15 minutes.

## NUTRITION

- Calories: 103
- Total Fat: 8.7g
- Saturated Fat: 4.1g
- Cholesterol: 25mg
- Sodium: 296mg

- Total Carbohydrate: 0.9g
- Dietary Fiber: 0.2g
- Total Sugars: 0.3g
- Protein: 5.2g
- Potassium: 93mg

**PREPARATION: 35 MIN**

**COOKING: 0 MIN**

**SERVES: 8**

# 30. BLT PARTY BITES

## INGREDIENTS

- 4 oz. bacon, chopped
- 3 tablespoons panko breadcrumbs
- 1 tablespoon Parmesan cheese, grated
- 1 teaspoon mayonnaise
- 1 teaspoon lemon juice
- Salt to taste
- ½ heart Romaine lettuce, shredded
- 6 cocktail tomatoes

## DIRECTIONS

1. Put the bacon in a pan over medium heat.
2. Fry until crispy.
3. Transfer bacon to a plate lined with paper towel.
4. Add breadcrumbs and cook until crunchy.
5. Transfer breadcrumbs to another plate also lined with paper towel.
6. Sprinkle Parmesan cheese on top of the breadcrumbs.
7. Mix the mayonnaise, salt and lemon juice.
8. Toss the Romaine in the mayo mixture.
9. Slice each tomato on the bottom to create a flat surface so it can stand by itself.
10. Slice the top off as well.
11. Scoop out the insides of the tomatoes.
12. Stuff each tomato with the bacon, Parmesan, breadcrumbs and top with the lettuce.

## NUTRITION

- Calories: 107
- Total Fat: 6.5g
- Saturated Fat: 2.1g
- Cholesterol: 16mg
- Sodium: 360mg

- Total Carbohydrate: 5.4g
- Dietary Fiber: 1.5g
- Total Sugars: 3.3g
- Protein: 6.5g
- Potassium: 372mg

# 10. LUNCH

**PREPARATION: 5 MIN**

**COOKING: 5 MIN**

**SERVES: 4**

# 31. BUTTERED COD

## INGREDIENTS

- 1 ½ lb. cod fillets, sliced
- 6 tablespoons butter, sliced
- ¼ teaspoon garlic powder
- ¾ teaspoon ground paprika
- Salt and pepper to taste
- Lemon slices
- Chopped parsley

## DIRECTIONS

1. Mix the garlic powder, paprika, salt and pepper in a bowl.
2. Season cod pieces with seasoning mixture.
3. Add 2 tablespoons butter in a pan over medium heat.
4. Let half of the butter melt.
5. Add the cod and cook for 2 minutes per side.
6. Top with the remaining slices of butter.
7. Cook for 3 to 4 minutes.
8. Garnish with parsley and lemon slices before serving.

## NUTRITION

- Calories: 295
- Total Fat: 19g
- Saturated Fat: 11g
- Cholesterol: 128mg
- Sodium: 236mg
- Total Carbohydrate: 1.5g
- Dietary Fiber: 0.7g
- Total Sugars: 0.3g
- Protein: 30.7g
- Potassium: 102mg

**PREPARATION: 10 MIN**

**COOKING: 22 MIN**

**SERVES: 4**

# 32. SALMON WITH RED CURRY SAUCE

## INGREDIENTS

- 4 salmon fillets
- 2 tablespoons olive oil
- Salt and pepper to taste
- 1 ½ tablespoons red curry paste
- 1 tablespoon fresh ginger, chopped
- 14 oz. coconut cream
- 1 ½ tablespoons fish sauce

## DIRECTIONS

1. Preheat your oven to 350 degrees F.
2. Cover baking sheet with foil.
3. Brush both sides of salmon fillets with olive oil and season with salt and pepper.
4. Place the salmon fillets on the baking sheet.
5. Bake salmon in the oven for 20 minutes.
6. In a pan over medium heat, mix the curry paste, ginger, coconut cream and fish sauce.
7. Sprinkle with salt and pepper.
8. Simmer for 2 minutes.
9. Pour the sauce over the salmon before serving.

## NUTRITION

- Calories: 553
- Total Fat: 43.4g
- Saturated Fat: 24.1g
- Cholesterol: 78mg
- Sodium: 908mg
- Total Carbohydrate: 7.9g
- Dietary Fiber: 2.4g
- Total Sugars: 3.6g
- Protein: 37.3g
- Potassium: 982mg

**PREPARATION: 15 MIN**

**COOKING: 25 MIN**

**SERVES: 6**

# 33. SALMON TERIYAKI

## INGREDIENTS

- 3 tablespoons sesame oil
- 2 teaspoons fish sauce
- 3 tablespoons coconut amino
- 2 teaspoons ginger, grated
- 4 garlic cloves, crushed
- 2 tablespoons xylitol
- 1 tablespoon green lime juice
- 2 teaspoons green lime zest
- Cayenne pepper to taste
- 6 salmon fillets
- 1 teaspoon arrowroot starch
- ¼ cup water
- Sesame seeds

## DIRECTIONS

1. Preheat your oven to 400 degrees F.
2. Combine the sesame oil, fish sauce, coconut amino, ginger, garlic, xylitol, green lime juice, zest and cayenne pepper in a mixing bowl.
3. Create 6 packets using foil.
4. Add half of the marinade in the packets.
5. Add the salmon inside.
6. Place in the baking sheet and cook for about 20 to 25 minutes.
7. Add the remaining sauce in a pan over medium heat.
8. Dissolve arrowroot in water, and add to the sauce.
9. Simmer until the sauce has thickened.
10. Place the salmon on a serving platter and pour the sauce on top.
11. Sprinkle sesame seeds on top before serving.

## NUTRITION

- Calories: 312
- Total Fat: 17.9g
- Saturated Fat: 2.6g
- Cholesterol: 78mg
- Sodium: 242mg
- Total Carbohydrate: 3.5g
- Dietary Fiber: 0.1g
- Total Sugars: 0.1g
- Protein: 34.8g
- Potassium: 706mg

**PREPARATION: 10 MIN**

**COOKING: 15 MIN**

**SERVES: 3**

# 34. PESTO SHRIMP WITH ZUCCHINI NOODLES

## INGREDIENTS

- Pesto sauce
- 3 cups basil leaves
- ¾ cup pine nuts
- 2 garlic cloves
- ½ lemon, juiced
- 1 teaspoon lemon zest
- Salt to taste
- ¼ cup olive oil
- Shrimp and Zoodles
- 3 zucchinis
- Salt to taste
- 1 lb. shrimp
- 2 tablespoons avocado oil

## DIRECTIONS

1. Put all the pesto ingredients in a blender.
2. Blend until smooth.
3. Spiralize the zucchini into noodle form.
4. Season with salt.
5. Drain water from the zucchini noodles.
6. Season the shrimp with salt and pepper.
7. Add half of the oil in a pan over medium heat.
8. Once the oil is hot, add the shrimp and cook for 1 to 2 minutes.
9. Add the remaining oil to the pan.
10. Add the zucchini noodles and cook for 3 minutes.
11. Add the pesto and toss to coat the noodles evenly with the sauce.
12. Season with salt.

## NUTRITION

- Calories: 304
- Total Fat: 22.2g
- Saturated Fat: 2.6g
- Cholesterol: 159mg
- Sodium: 223mg
- Total Carbohydrate: 8g
- Dietary Fiber: 2.3g
- Total Sugars: 2.5g
- Protein: 21.3g
- Potassium: 547mg

# 35. CRAB CAKES

## INGREDIENTS

- 2 tablespoons butter
- 2 garlic cloves, minced
- ½ cup bell pepper, chopped
- 1 rib celery, chopped
- 1 shallot, chopped
- Salt and pepper to taste
- 2 tablespoons mayonnaise
- 1 egg, beaten
- 1 teaspoon mustard
- 1 tablespoon Worcestershire sauce
- 1 teaspoon hot sauce
- ½ cup Parmesan cheese, grated
- ½ cup pork rinds, crushed
- 1 lb. crabmeat
- 2 tablespoons olive oil

## DIRECTIONS

1. Add the butter to the pan over medium heat.
2. Add the garlic, bell pepper, celery, shallot, salt and pepper.
3. Cook for 10 minutes.
4. In a bowl, mix the mayo, egg, Worcestershire, mustard and hot sauce.
5. Add the sautéed vegetables to this mixture.
6. Mix well.
7. Add the cheese and pork rind.
8. Fold in the crabmeat.
9. Line the baking sheet with foil.
10. Create patties from the mixture.
11. Place the patties on the baking sheet.
12. Cover the baking sheet with foil.
13. Refrigerate for 1 hour.
14. Fry in olive oil in a pan over medium heat.
15. Cook until crispy and golden brown.

### NUTRITION

- Calories: 150
- Total Fat: 9.2g
- Saturated Fat: 3.2g
- Cholesterol: 43mg
- Sodium: 601mg
- Total Carbohydrate: 10.8g
- Dietary Fiber: 0.5g
- Total Sugars: 4.6g
- Protein: 6.4g
- Potassium: 80mg

**PREPARATION: 5 MIN**

**COOKING: 0 MIN**

**SERVES: 2**

# 36. TUNA SALAD

## INGREDIENTS

- 1 cup tuna flakes
- 3 tablespoons mayonnaise
- 1 teaspoon onion flakes
- Salt and pepper to taste
- 3 cups Romaine lettuce

## DIRECTIONS

1. Mix the tuna flakes, mayonnaise, onion flakes, salt and pepper in a bowl.
2. Serve with lettuce.

## NUTRITION

- Calories: 130
- Total Fat: 7.8g
- Saturated Fat: 1.1g
- Cholesterol: 13mg
- Sodium: 206mg
- Total Carbohydrate: 8.5g
- Dietary Fiber: 0.6g
- Total Sugars: 2.6g
- Protein: 8.2g
- Potassium: 132mg

**PREPARATION: 15 MIN**

**COOKING: 0 MIN**

**SERVES: 1**

# 37. KETO SHAKE

## INGREDIENTS

- ¾ cup almond milk
- ½ cup ice
- 2 tablespoons almond butter
- 2 tablespoons cocoa powder (unsweetened)
- 2 tablespoons Swerve
- 1 tablespoon chia seeds
- 2 tablespoons hemp seeds
- ½ tablespoon vanilla extract
- Salt to taste

## DIRECTIONS

1. Blend all the ingredients in a food processor.
2. Chill in the refrigerator before serving.

## NUTRITION

- Calories: 104
- Total Fat: 9.5g
- Saturated Fat: 5.1g
- Cholesterol: 0mg
- Sodium: 24mg
- Total Carbohydrate: 3.6g
- Dietary Fiber: 1.4g
- Total Sugars: 1.1g
- Protein: 2.9g
- Potassium: 159mg

**PREPARATION: 30 MIN**

**COOKING: 0 MIN**

**SERVES: 10**

# 38. KETO FAT BOMBS

## INGREDIENTS

- 8 tablespoons butter
- ¼ cup Swerve
- ½ teaspoon vanilla extract
- Salt to taste
- 2 cups almond flour
- 2/3 cup chocolate chips

## DIRECTIONS

1. In a bowl, beat the butter until fluffy.
2. Stir in the sugar, salt and vanilla.
3. Mix well.
4. Add the almond flour.
5. Fold in the chocolate chips.
6. Cover the bowl with cling wrap and refrigerate for 20 minutes.
7. Create balls from the dough.

## NUTRITION

- Calories: 176
- Total Fat: 15.2g
- Saturated Fat: 8.4g
- Cholesterol: 27mg
- Sodium: 92mg
- Total Carbohydrate: 12.9g
- Dietary Fiber: 1g
- Total Sugars: 10.8g
- Protein: 2.2g
- Potassium: 45mg

**PREPARATION: 20 MIN**

**COOKING: 0 MIN**

**SERVES: 10**

# 39. AVOCADO ICE POPS

## INGREDIENTS

- 3 avocados
- ¼ cup lime juice
- 3 tablespoons Swerve
- ¾ cup coconut milk
- 1 tablespoon coconut oil
- 1 cup keto friendly chocolate

## DIRECTIONS

1. Add all the ingredients except the oil and chocolate in a blender.
2. Blend until smooth.
3. Pour the mixture into the popsicle mold.
4. Freeze overnight.
5. In a bowl, mix oil and chocolate chips.
6. Melt in the microwave. And then let cool.
7. Dunk the avocado popsicles into the chocolate before serving

## NUTRITION

- Calories: 176
- Total Fat: 17.4g
- Saturated Fat: 7.5g
- Cholesterol: 0mg
- Sodium: 6mg

- Total Carbohydrate: 10.8g
- Dietary Fiber: 4.5g
- Total Sugars: 5.4g
- Protein: 1.6g
- Potassium: 341mg

**PREPARATION: 1H 10**

**COOKING: 0 MIN**

**SERVES: 8**

# 40. CARROT BALLS

## INGREDIENTS

- 8 oz. block cream cheese
- ¾ cup coconut flour
- ½ teaspoon pure vanilla extract
- 1 teaspoon stevia
- ¼ teaspoon ground nutmeg
- 1 teaspoon cinnamon
- 1 cup carrots, grated
- 1/2 cup pecans, chopped
- 1 cup coconut, shredded

## DIRECTIONS

1. Use a hand mixer to beat the cream cheese, coconut flour, vanilla, stevia, nutmeg and cinnamon.
2. Fold in the carrots and pecans.
3. Form into balls.
4. Refrigerate for 1 hour.
5. Roll into shredded coconut before serving.

## NUTRITION

- Calories: 390
- Total Fat: 35g
- Saturated Fat: 17g
- Cholesterol: 60mg
- Sodium: 202mg
- Total Carbohydrate: 17.2g
- Dietary Fiber: 7.8g
- Total Sugars: 6g
- Protein: 7.8g
- Potassium: 154mg

**PREPARATION: 2 MIN**

**COOKING: 30 MIN**

**SERVES: 20**

# 41. COCONUT CRACK BARS

## INGREDIENTS

- 3 cups coconut flakes (unsweetened)
- 1 cup coconut oil
- ¼ cup maple syrup

## DIRECTIONS

1. Line a baking sheet with parchment paper.
2. Put coconut in a bowl.
3. Add the oil and syrup.
4. Mix well.
5. Pour the mixture into the pan.
6. Refrigerate until firm.
7. Slice into bars before serving.

## NUTRITION

- Calories: 147
- Total Fat: 14.9g
- Saturated Fat: 13g
- Cholestero: 0mg
- Sodium: 3mg
- Total Carbohydrate: 4.5g
- Dietary Fiber: 1.1g
- Total Sugars: 3.1g
- Protein: 0.4g
- Potassium: 51mg

**PREPARATION: 1H 20**

**COOKING: 0 MIN**

**SERVES: 4**

# 42. STRAWBERRY ICE CREAM

## INGREDIENTS

- 17 oz. coconut milk
- 16 oz. frozen strawberries
- ¾ cup Swerve
- ½ cup fresh strawberries

## DIRECTIONS

1. Put all the ingredients except fresh strawberries in a blender.
2. Pulse until smooth.
3. Put the mixture in an ice cream maker.
4. Use ice cream maker according to directions.
5. Add the fresh strawberries a few minutes before the ice cream is done.
6. Freeze for 1 hour before serving.

## NUTRITION

- Calories: 320
- Total Fat: 28.8g
- Saturated Fat: 25.5g
- Cholesterol: 0mg
- Sodium: 18mg
- Total Carbohydrate: 25.3g
- Dietary Fiber: 5.3g
- Total Sugars: 19.1g
- Protein: 2.9g
- Potassium: 344mg

# 43. KEY LIME PUDDING

## INGREDIENTS

- 1 cup hot water
- 2/4 cup erythrytol syrup
- 6 drops stevia
- 1 teaspoon almond extract
- 1 teaspoon vanilla extract
- ¼ teaspoon Xanthan gum powder
- 2 ripe avocados, sliced
- 1 ½ oz. lime juice
- 3 tablespoons coconut oil
- Salt to taste

## DIRECTIONS

1. Add water, erythritol, stevia, almond extract and vanilla extract to a pot.
2. Bring to a boil.
3. Simmer until the syrup has been reduced and has thickened.
4. Turn the heat off.
5. Add the gum powder.
6. Mix until thickened.
7. Add the avocado into a food processor.
8. Add the rest of the ingredients.
9. Pulse until smooth.
10. Place the mixture in ramekins.
11. Refrigerate for 1 hour.
12. Pour the syrup over the pudding before serving.

## NUTRITION

- Calories: 299
- Total Fat: 29.8g
- Saturated Fat: 12.9g
- Cholesterol: 0mg
- Sodium: 47mg
- Total Carbohydrate: 9.7g
- Dietary Fiber: 6.8g
- Total Sugars: 0.8g
- Protein: 2g
- Potassium: 502mg

**PREPARATION: 10 MIN**

**COOKING: 15 MIN**

**SERVES: 4**

# 44. CHICKEN IN SWEET AND SOUR SAUCE WITH CORN SALAD

## INGREDIENTS

- 2 cups plus 2 tablespoons of unflavored low-fat yoghurt
- 2 cups of frozen mango chunks
- 3 tablespoons of honey
- ¼ cup plus 1 tablespoon apple cider vinegar
- ¼ cup sultana
- 2 tablespoons of olive oil, plus an amount to be brushed
- ¼ teaspoon of cayenne pepper
- 5 dried tomatoes (not in oil)
- 2 small garlic cloves, finely chopped
- 4 cobs, peeled
- 8 peeled and boned chicken legs, peeled (about 700g)
- 6 cups of mixed salad
- 2 medium carrots, finely sliced

## DIRECTIONS

1. For the smoothie: in a blender, mix 2 cups of yogurt, 2 cups of ice, 1 cup of mango and all the honey until the mixture becomes completely smooth. Divide into 4glasses and refrigerate until ready to use. Rinse the blender.
2. Preheat the grill to medium-high heat. Mix the remaining cup of mango, ¼ cup water, ¼ cup vinegar, sultanas, olive oil, cayenne pepper, tomatoes and garlic in a microwave bowl. Cover with a piece of clear film and cook in the microwave until the tomatoes become soft, for about 3 minutes. Leave to cool slightly and pass in a blender. Transfer to a small bowl. Leave 2 tablespoons aside to garnish, turn the chicken into the remaining mixture.
3. Put the corn on the grill, cover and bake, turning it over if necessary, until it is burnt, about 10 minutes. Remove and keep warm.
4. Brush the grill over medium heat and brush the grills with a little oil. Turn the chicken legs into half the remaining sauce and ½ teaspoon of salt. Put on the grill and cook until the cooking marks appear and the internal temperature reaches 75°C on an instantaneous thermometer, 8 to 10 minutes per side. Bart and sprinkle a few times with the remaining sauce while cooking.
5. While the chicken is cooking, beat the remaining 2 tablespoons of yogurt, the 2 tablespoons of sauce set aside, the remaining spoonful of vinegar, 1 tablespoon of water and ¼ teaspoon of salt in a large bowl. Mix the mixed salad with the carrots. Divide chicken, corn and salad into 4 serving dishes. Garnish the salad with the dressing set aside. Serve each plate with a mango smoothie.

## NUTRITION

- Calories: 346
- Protein: 56g
- Fat: 45g

# 45. CHINESE CHICKEN SALAD

## INGREDIENTS

**For the chicken salad:**
- 4 divided chicken breasts with skin and bones
- Olive oil of excellent quality
- Salt and freshly ground black pepper
- 500g asparagus, with the ends removed and cut into three parts diagonally
- 1 red pepper, peeled
- Chinese condiment, recipe to follow
- 2 spring onions (both the white and the green part), sliced diagonally
- 1 tablespoon of white sesame seeds, toasted

**For Chinese dressing:**
- 120 ml vegetable oil
- 60 ml of apple cider vinegar of excellent quality
- 60 ml soy sauce
- 1 ½ tablespoon of black sesame
- ½ tablespoon of honey
- 1 garlic clove, minced
- ½ teaspoon of fresh peeled and grated ginger
- ½ tablespoon sesame seeds, toasted
- 60g peanut butter
- 2 teaspoons of salt
- ½ teaspoons freshly ground black pepper

## DIRECTIONS

1. For the chicken salad:
2. Heat the oven to 180°C (or 200°C for gas oven). Put the chicken breast on a baking tray and rub the skin with a little olive oil. Season freely with salt and pepper.
3. Brown for 35 to 40 minutes, until the chicken is freshly cooked. Let it cool down as long as it takes to handle it. Remove the meat from the bones, remove the skin and chop the chicken into medium-sized pieces.
4. Blanch the asparagus in a pot of salted water for 3-5 minutes until tender. Soak them in water with ice to stop cooking. Drain them. Cut the peppers into strips the same size as the asparagus. In a large bowl, mix the chopped chicken, asparagus and peppers.
5. Spread the Chinese dressing on chicken and vegetables. Add the spring onions and sesame seeds, and season to taste. Serve cold or at room temperature.
6. For Chinese dressing:
7. Mix all ingredients and set aside until use.

## NUTRITION

- Calories: 222
- Protein: 28g
- Fat: 10g
- Sugar: 6g

**PREPARATION: 15 MIN**

**COOKING: 25 MIN**

**SERVES: 4**

# 46. CHICKEN SALAD

## INGREDIENTS

**For the Buffalo chicken salad:**
- 2 chicken breasts (225g) peeled, boned, cut in half
- 2 tablespoons of hot cayenne pepper sauce (or another type of hot sauce), plus an addition depending on taste
- 2 tablespoons of olive oil
- 2 romaine lettuce heart, cut into 2 cm strips
- 4 celery stalks, finely sliced
- 2 carrots, roughly grated
- 2 fresh onions, only the green part, sliced
- 125 ml of blue cheese dressing, recipe to follow

**For the seasoning of blue cheese:**
- 2 tablespoons mayonnaise
- 70 ml of partially skimmed buttermilk
- 70 ml low-fat white yoghurt
- 1 tablespoon of wine vinegar
- ½ teaspoon of sugar
- 35g of chopped blue cheese
- Salt and freshly ground black pepper

## DIRECTIONS

1. For the Buffalo chicken salad:
2. Preheat the grid.
3. Place the chicken between 2 sheets of baking paper and beat it with a meat tenderizer so that it is about 2 cm thick, then cut the chicken sideways creating 1 cm strips.
4. In a large bowl, add the hot sauce and oil, add the chicken and turn it over until it is well soaked. Place the chicken on a baking tray and grill until well cooked, about 4-6 minutes, turning it once.
5. In a large bowl, add the lettuce, celery, grated carrots and fresh onions. Add the seasoning of blue cheese. Distribute the vegetables in 4 plates and arrange the chicken on each of the dishes. Serve with hot sauce on the side.
6. For the blue cheese dressing:
7. Cover a small bowl with absorbent paper folded in four. Spread the yoghurt on the paper and put it in the fridge for 20 minutes to drain and firm it.
8. In a medium bowl, beat the buttermilk and firm yogurt with mayonnaise until well blended. Add the vinegar and sugar and keep beating until well blended. Add the blue cheese and season with salt and pepper to taste.

## NUTRITION

- Calories: 321
- Fat: 3g
- Fiber: 5g
- Carbs: 7g
- Protein: 4g

90

**PREPARATION: 15 MIN**

**COOKING: 20 MIN**

**SERVES: 3**

# 47. TOFU MEAT AND SALAD

## INGREDIENTS

- 1 tablespoon of garlic sauce and chili in a bottle
- 1 1/2 tablespoon sesame oil
- 3 tablespoons of low-sodium soy sauce
- 60 ml hoisin sauce
- 2 tablespoons rice vinegar
- 2 tablespoons of sherry or Chinese cooking wine
- 225g of extra-solid tofu
- 2 teaspoons of rapeseed oil
- 2 tablespoons of finely chopped fresh ginger
- 4 spring onions, with the green part chopped and set aside, in thin slices
- 225g of minced lean beef (90% or more lean)
- 25g of diced Chinese water chestnuts
- 1 large head of cappuccino lettuce, with the leaves separated, but without the outer ones
- 1 red pepper, diced

## DIRECTIONS

1. In a bowl, mix together the garlic and chili sauce, sesame oil, soy sauce, hoisin sauce, vinegar and sherry.
2. Cut the tofu into 1 cm thick slices and place them on a kitchen towel. Use the cloth to dab the tofu well to remove as much water as possible. Should take a couple of minutes and about three dish towels. Chop the dry tofu well and set aside.
3. Heat the oil in a wok or in a very large pan in medium flame. Add the ginger and the white part of the spring onions and cook until the spring onions become translucent and the ginger fragrant, for about 2-3 minutes. Add the beef and tofu and cook, stirring, until the meat becomes dull and freshly cooked, for about 4-5 minutes. Add the sauce set aside. Reduce the flame and simmer slowly, stirring, for another 3-4 minutes. Add the chestnuts and mix well to incorporate.
4. Fill each lettuce leaf with stuffing. Serve by decorating with the green part of the spring onions, red pepper and peanuts.

## NUTRITION

- Calories: 122
- Fat: 2g
- Protein: 66g

**PREPARATION: 10 MIN**

**COOKING: 5 MIN**

**SERVES: 2**

# 48. ASPARAGUS AND PISTACHIOS VINAIGRETTE

## INGREDIENTS

- Two 455g bunches of large asparagus, without the tip
- 1 tablespoon of olive oil
- Salt and freshly ground black pepper
- 6 tablespoons of sliced pistachios blanched and boiled
- 1 ½ tablespoon lemon juice
- 1/4 teaspoon of sugar
- 1 ½ teaspoon lemon zest

## DIRECTIONS

1. Preheat the oven to 220°C. Put the grill in the top third of the oven. Place the asparagus on a baking tray covered with baking paper. Sprinkle with olive oil and season with a little salt and pepper. Bake for 15 minutes, until soft.
2. Meanwhile, blend 5 tablespoons of almonds, lemon juice, sugar and 6 tablespoons of water for 1 minute until smooth. Taste and regulate salt. Pour the sauce on a plate and put the spinach on the sauce. Decorate with peel and the remaining spoon of pistachios

## NUTRITION

- Calories: 560
- Fat: 5g
- Fiber: 2g

- Carbs: 3g
- Protein: 9g

**PREPARATION: 30 MIN**

**COOKING: 0 MIN**

**SERVES: 4**

# 49. TURKEY MEATBALLS

## INGREDIENTS

- 255g turkey sausage
- 2 tablespoons of extra virgin olive oil
- One can of 425g chickpeas, rinsed and drained...
- ½ medium onion, chopped, 2/3 cup
- 2 garlic cloves, finely chopped
- 1 teaspoon of cumin
- ½ cup flour
- ½ teaspoon instant yeast for desserts
- Salt and ground black pepper
- 1 cup of Greek yogurt
- 2 tablespoons of lime juice
- 2 radicchio hearts, chopped
- Hot sauce

## DIRECTIONS

1. Preheat the oven to 200°C.
2. In a processor, blend the chickpeas, onion, garlic, cumin, 1 teaspoon salt and 1/2 teaspoon pepper until all the ingredients are finely chopped. Add the flour, baking powder and blend to make everything mix well. Transfer to a medium bowl and add the sausage, stirring together with your hands. Cover and refrigerate for 30 minutes.
3. Once cold, take the mixture in spoonful, forming 1-inch balls with wet hands. Heat the olive oil in a pan over medium heat. In two groups, put the falafel in the pan and cook until slightly brown, about a minute and a half per side. Transfer to a baking tray and bake in the oven until well cooked, for about 10 minutes.
4. Mix together the yogurt, lime juice, 1/2 teaspoon salt and 1/4 teaspoon pepper. Divide the lettuce into 4 plates, season with some yogurt sauce.

## NUTRITION

- Calories: 189
- Fat: 5g
- Protein: 77g

- Sugar: 3g

**PREPARATION: 5 MIN**

**COOKING: 30 MIN**

**SERVES: 8**

# 50. ORANGE FRENCH TOAST

## INGREDIENTS

- 2 cups of plant milk (unflavored)
- Four tablespoon maple syrup
- 1 ½ tablespoon cinnamon
- Salt (optional)
- 1 cup flour (almond)
- 1 tablespoon orange zest
- 8 bread slices

## DIRECTIONS

1. Turn the oven and heat to 400 degree F afterwards.
2. In a cup, add ingredients and whisk until the batter is smooth.
3. Dip each piece of bread into the paste and permit to soak for a couple of seconds.
4. Put in the pan, and cook until lightly browned.
5. Put the toast on the cookie sheet and bake for ten to fifteen minutes in the oven, until it is crispy.

## NUTRITION

- Calories: 129
- Fat: 1.1g
- Carbohydrates: 21.5g
- Protein: 7.9g

**PREPARATION: 50 MIN**

**COOKING: 30 MIN**

**SERVES: 8**

# 51. CHOCOLATE CHIP COCONUT PANCAKES

## INGREDIENTS

- 1 ¼ cup oats
- 2 teaspoons coconut flakes
- 2 cup plant milk
- 1 ¼ cup maple syrup
- 1 1/3 cup of chocolate chips
- 2 ¼ cups buckwheat flour
- 2 teaspoon baking powder
- 1 teaspoon vanilla essence
- 2 teaspoon flaxseed meal
- Salt (optional)

## DIRECTIONS

1. Put the flaxseed and cook over medium heat until the paste becomes a little moist.
2. Remove seeds.
3. Stir the buckwheat, oats, coconut chips, baking powder and salt with each other in a wide dish.
4. In a large dish, stir together the retained flax water with the sugar, maple syrup, vanilla essence.
5. Transfer the wet mixture to the dry ingredients and shake to combine
6. Place over medium heat the nonstick grill pan.
7. Pour 1/4 cup flour onto the grill pan with each pancake, and scatter gently.
8. Cook for five to six minutes, before the pancakes appear somewhat crispy.

## NUTRITION

- Calories: 198
- Fat: 9.1g
- Carbohydrates: 11.5g

- Protein: 7.9g

**PREPARATION: 10 MIN**

**COOKING: 30 MIN**

**SERVES: 3**

# 52. CHICKPEA OMELET

## INGREDIENTS

- 2 cup flour (chickpea)
- 1 ½ teaspoon onion powder
- 1 ½ teaspoon garlic powder
- ¼ teaspoon pepper (white and black)
- 1/3 cup yeast
- 1 teaspoon baking powder
- 3 green onions (chopped)

## DIRECTIONS

1. In a cup, add the chickpea flour and spices.
2. Apply 1 cup of sugar, then stir.
3. Power medium-heat and put the frying pan.
4. On each omelets, add onions and mushrooms in the batter while it heats.
5. Serve your delicious Chickpea Omelet.

## NUTRITION

- Calories: 399
- Fat: 11.1g
- Carbohydrates: 11.5g
- Protein: 7.9g

**PREPARATION: 5 MIN**

**COOKING: 15 MIN**

**SERVES: 1-2**

# 53. APPLE-LEMON BOWL

## INGREDIENTS

- 6 apples
- 3 tablespoons walnuts
- 7 dates
- Lemon juice
- ½ teaspoon cinnamon

## DIRECTIONS

1. Root the apples, then break them into wide bits.
2. In a food cup, put seeds, part of the lime juice, almonds, spices and three-quarters of the apples. Thinly slice until finely ground.
3. Apply the remaining apples and lemon juice and make slices.

## NUTRITION

- Calories: 249
- Fat: 5.1g
- Carbohydrates: 71.5g
- Protein: 7.9g

**PREPARATION: 10 MIN**

**COOKING: 30 MIN**

**SERVES: 6**

# 54. BREAKFAST SCRAMBLE

## INGREDIENTS

- 1 red onion
- 2 tablespoons soy sauce
- 2 cups sliced mushrooms
- Salt to taste
- 1 ½ teaspoon black pepper
- 1 ½ teaspoons turmeric
- ¼ teaspoon cayenne
- 3 garlic cloves
- 1 red bell pepper
- 1 large head cauliflower
- 1 green bell pepper

## DIRECTIONS

1. In a small pan, put all vegetables and cook until crispy.
2. Stir in the cauliflower and cook for four to six minutes or until it smooth.
3. Add spices to the pan and cook for another five minutes.

## NUTRITION

- Calories: 199
- Fat: 1.1g
- Carbohydrates: 14.5g
- Protein: 7.9g

**PREPARATION: 10 MIN**

**COOKING: 30 MIN**

**SERVES: 4**

# 55. BLACK BEAN AND SWEET POTATO HASH

## INGREDIENTS

- 1 cup onion (chopped)
- 1/3 Cup vegetable broth
- 2 garlic (minced)
- 1 cup cooked black beans
- 2 teaspoons hot chili powder
- 2 cups chopped sweet potatoes

## DIRECTIONS

1. Put the onions in a saucepan over medium heat and add the seasoning and mix.
2. Add potatoes and chili flakes, then mix.
3. Cook for around 12 minutes more until the vegetables are cooked thoroughly.
4. Add the green onion, beans, and salt
5. Cook for more 2 minutes and serve.

## NUTRITION

- Calories: 239
- Fat: 1.1g
- Carbohydrates: 71.5g
- Protein: 7.9g

**PREPARATION: 15 MIN**

**COOKING: 60 MIN**

**SERVES: 8**

# 56. APPLE-WALNUT BREAKFAST BREAD

## INGREDIENTS

- 1 ½ cups apple sauce
- 1/3 cup plant milk
- 2 cups all-purpose flour
- Salt to taste
- 1 teaspoon ground cinnamon
- 1 tablespoon flax seeds mixed with 2 tablespoons warm water
- ¾ cup brown sugar
- 1 teaspoon baking powder
- ½ cup chopped walnuts

## DIRECTIONS

1. Preheat to 375 degree Fahrenheit.
2. Combine the apple sauce, sugar, milk, and flax mixture in a jar and mix.
3. Combine the flour, baking powder, salt, and cinnamon in a separate bowl.
4. Simply add dry ingredients into the wet ingredients and combine to make slices.
5. Bake for 25 minutes until it becomes light brown.

## NUTRITION

- Calories: 309
- Fat: 9.1g
- Carbohydrates: 16.5g
- Protein: 6.9g

**PREPARATION: 10 MIN**

**COOKING: 30 MIN**

**SERVES: 2**

# 57. VEGAN SALMON BAGEL

## INGREDIENTS

- 4 cups of water
- 1 ½ red onion
- Vegan cream cheese
- Salt, pepper
- 4 bagels
- 1 ½ cup of apple cider vinegar
- 7 carrots

## DIRECTIONS

1. Preheat to 200 degree Celsius.
2. Slice the carrots.
3. In a mixer to mix, combine sugar, vinegar, and ground pepper.
4. Put the carrot strips in a stir fry bowl, apply the marinade and stir.
5. Cover the carrots with foil and bake for twenty minutes, then switch heat down to 210°F and cook for 40 minutes more.

## NUTRITION

- Calories: 232
- Fat: 9.1g
- Carbohydrates: 71.5g
- Protein: 7.9g

**PREPARATION: 5 MIN**

**COOKING: 10 MIN**

**SERVES: 1**

# 58. MINT CHOCOLATE GREEN PROTEIN SMOOTHIE

## INGREDIENTS

- 1 scoop chocolate powder
- 1 tablespoon flaxseed
- 1 banana
- 1 mint leaf
- ¾ cup almond milk
- 3 tablespoons dark chocolate (chopped)

## DIRECTIONS

1. Blend all the ingredients except the dark chocolate.
2. Garnish dark chocolate when ready.

## NUTRITION

- Calories: 300
- Fat: 19.1g
- Carbohydrates: 21.5g
- Protein: 27.9g

**PREPARATION: 5 MIN**

**COOKING: 10 MIN**

**SERVES: 2**

# 59. DAIRY-FREE COCONUT YOGURT

## INGREDIENTS

- 1 can coconut milk
- 4 vegan probiotic capsules

## DIRECTIONS

1. Shake coconut milk with a whole tube.
2. Remove the plastic of capsules and mix in.
3. Cut a 12-inch cheesecloth until stirred.
4. Freeze or eat immediately.

## NUTRITION

- Calories: 219
- Fat: 10.1g
- Carbohydrates: 1.5g
- Protein: 7.9g

**PREPARATION: 5 MIN**

**COOKING: 10 MIN**

**SERVES: 2**

# 60. VEGAN GREEN AVOCADO SMOOTHIE

## INGREDIENTS

- 1 banana
- 1 cup water
- ½ avocado
- ½ lemon juice
- ½ cup coconut yoghurt

## DIRECTIONS

**1.** Blend all ingredients until smooth.

## NUTRITION

- Calories: 299
- Fat: 1.1g
- Carbohydrates: 1.5g

- Protein: 7.9g

**PREPARATION: 10 MIN**

**COOKING: 35 MIN**

**SERVES: 12 CUPS**

# 61. SUN-BUTTER BAKED OATMEAL CUPS

## INGREDIENTS

- ¼ cup coconut sugar
- 1 ½ rolled oats
- 2 tablespoon chia seeds
- ¼ teaspoon salt
- 1 teaspoon cinnamon
- ½ cup non-dairy milk
- ½ cup Sun-Butter
- ½ cup apple sauce

## DIRECTIONS

1. Preheat oven to 350°F.
2. Mix all ingredients and blend well.
3. Add in muffins and Insert extra toppings.
4. Bake 25 minutes, or until golden brown.

## NUTRITION

- Calories: 129
- Fat: 1.1g
- Carbohydrates: 1.5g
- Protein: 4.9g

# 11. DINNER

**PREPARATION: 20 MIN**

**COOKING: 25 MIN**

**SERVES: 4**

# 62. BEEF-STUFFED MUSHROOMS

## INGREDIENTS

- 4 mushrooms, stemmed
- 3 tablespoons olive oil, divided
- 1 yellow onion, sliced thinly
- 1 red bell pepper, sliced into strips
- 1 green bell pepper, sliced into strips
- Salt and pepper to taste
- 8 oz. beef, sliced thinly
- 3 oz. provolone cheese, sliced
- Chopped parsley

## DIRECTIONS

1. Preheat your oven to 350 degrees F.
2. Arrange the mushrooms on a baking pan.
3. Brush with oil.
4. Add the remaining oil to a pan over medium heat.
5. Cook onion and bell peppers for 5 minutes.
6. Season with salt and pepper.
7. Place onion mixture on a plate.
8. Cook the beef in the pan for 5 minutes.
9. Sprinkle with salt and pepper.
10. Add the onion mixture back to the pan.
11. Mix well.
12. Fill the mushrooms with the beef mixture and cheese.
13. Bake in the oven for 15 minutes.

## NUTRITION

- Calories: 333
- Total Fat: 20.3g
- Saturated Fat: 6.7g
- Cholesterol: 61 mg
- Sodium: 378 mg
- Total Carbohydrate: 8.2g
- Dietary Fiber: 3.7g
- Protein: 25.2g
- Total Sugars: 7g
- Potassium: 789 mg

**PREPARATION: 15 MIN**

**COOKING: 3 HOURS**

**SERVES: 8**

# 63. RIB ROAST

## INGREDIENTS

- 1 rib roast
- Salt to taste
- 12 garlic cloves, chopped
- 2 teaspoons lemon zest
- 6 tablespoons fresh rosemary, chopped
- 5 sprigs thyme

## DIRECTIONS

1. Preheat your oven to 325 degrees F.
2. Season all sides of rib roast with salt.
3. Place the rib roast in a baking pan.
4. Sprinkle with garlic, lemon zest and rosemary.
5. Add herb sprigs on top.
6. Roast for 3 hours.
7. Let rest for a few minutes and then slice and serve.

## NUTRITION

- Calories: 329
- Total Fat: 27g
- Saturated Fat: 9g
- Cholesterol: 59mg
- Sodium: 498mg
- Total Carbohydrate: 5.3g
- Dietary Fiber: 1.8g
- Protein: 18g
- Total Sugars: 2g
- Potassium: 493mg

# 64. BEEF STIR FRY

## INGREDIENTS

- 1 tablespoon soy sauce
- 1 tablespoon ginger, minced
- 1 teaspoon cornstarch
- 1 teaspoon dry sherry
- 12 oz. beef, sliced into strips
- 1 teaspoon toasted sesame oil
- 2 tablespoons oyster sauce
- 1 lb. baby bok choy, sliced
- 3 tablespoons chicken broth

## DIRECTIONS

1. Mix soy sauce, ginger, cornstarch and dry sherry in a bowl.
2. Toss the beef in the mixture.
3. Pour oil into a pan over medium heat.
4. Cook the beef for 5 minutes, stirring.
5. Add oyster sauce, bok choy and chicken broth to the pan.
6. Cook for 1 minute.

## NUTRITION

- Calories: 247
- Total Fat: 15.8g
- Saturated Fat: 4g
- Cholesterol: 69mg

- Sodium: 569mg
- Total Carbohydrate: 6.3g
- Dietary Fiber: 1.1g
- Protein: 25g

**PREPARATION: 15 MIN**

**COOKING: 15 MIN**

**SERVES: 4**

# 65. SWEET & SOUR PORK

## INGREDIENTS

- 1 lb. pork chops
- Salt and pepper to taste
- ½ cup sesame seeds
- 2 tablespoons peanut oil
- 2 tablespoons soy sauce
- 3 tablespoons apricot jam
- Chopped scallions

## DIRECTIONS

1. Season pork chops with salt and pepper.
2. Press sesame seeds on both sides of pork.
3. Pour oil into a pan over medium heat.
4. Cook pork for 3 to 5 minutes per side.
5. Transfer to a plate.
6. In a bowl, mix soy sauce and apricot jam.
7. Simmer for 3 minutes.
8. Pour sauce over the pork and garnish with scallions before serving.

## NUTRITION

- Calories: 414
- Total Fat: 27.5g
- Saturated Fat: 5.6g
- Cholesterol: 68mg
- Sodium: 607mg
- Total Carbohydrate: 12.9g
- Dietary Fiber: 1.8g
- Protein: 29g
- Total Sugars: 9g
- Potassium: 332mg

**PREPARATION: 30 MIN**

**COOKING: 15 MIN**

**SERVES: 4**

# 66. GRILLED PORK WITH SALSA

## INGREDIENTS

**Salsa:**
- 1 onion, chopped
- 1 tomato, chopped
- 1 peach, chopped
- 1 apricot, chopped
- 1 tablespoon olive oil
- 1 tablespoon lime juice
- 2 tablespoons fresh cilantro, chopped
- Salt and pepper to taste

**Pork:**
- 1 lb. pork tenderloin, sliced
- 1 tablespoon olive oil
- Salt and pepper to taste
- ½ teaspoon ground cumin
- ¾ teaspoon chili powder

## DIRECTIONS

1. Combine salsa ingredients in a bowl.
2. Cover and refrigerate.
3. Brush pork tenderloin with oil.
4. Season with salt, pepper, cumin and chili powder.
5. Grill pork for 5 to 7 minutes per side.
6. Slice pork and serve with salsa.

## NUTRITION

- Calories: 219
- Total Fat: 9.5g
- Saturated Fat: 1.8g
- Cholesterol: 74mg
- Sodium: 512mg
- Total Carbohydrate: 8.3g
- Dietary Fiber: 1.5g
- Protein: 24g
- Total Sugars: 6g
- Potassium 600mg

**PREPARATION: 15 MIN**

**COOKING: 1 HOUR**

**SERVES: 6**

# 67. GARLIC PORK LOIN

## INGREDIENTS

- 1 ½ lb. pork loin roast
- 4 garlic cloves, sliced into slivers
- Salt and pepper to taste

## DIRECTIONS

1. Preheat your oven to 425 degrees F.
2. Make several slits all over the pork roast.
3. Insert garlic slivers.
4. Sprinkle with salt and pepper.
5. Roast in the oven for 1 hour.

## NUTRITION

- Calories: 235
- Total Fat: 13.3g
- Saturated Fat: 2.6g
- Cholesterol: 71mg
- Sodium: 450mg
- Total Carbohydrate: 1.7g
- Dietary Fiber: 0.3g
- Protein: 25.7g
- Total Sugars: 3g
- Potassium: 383mg

**PREPARATION: 15 MIN**

**COOKING: 25 MIN**

**SERVES: 4**

# 68. CHICKEN PESTO

## INGREDIENTS

- 1 lb. chicken cutlet
- Salt and pepper to taste
- 1 tablespoon olive oil
- ½ cup onion, chopped
- ½ cup heavy cream
- ½ cup dry white wine
- 1 tomato, chopped
- ¼ cup pesto
- 2 tablespoons basil, chopped

## DIRECTIONS

1. Season chicken with salt and pepper.
2. Pour oil into a pan over medium heat.
3. Cook chicken for 3 to 4 minutes per side.
4. Place the chicken on a plate.
5. Add the onion to the pan.
6. Cook for 1 minute.
7. Stir in the rest of the ingredients.
8. Bring to a boil.
9. Simmer for 15 minutes.
10. Put the chicken back to the pan.
11. Cook for 2 more minutes and then serve.

## NUTRITION

- Calories: 371
- Total Fat: 23.7g
- Saturated Fat: 9.2g
- Cholesterol: 117mg
- Sodium: 361 mg
- Total Carbohydrate: 5.7g
- Dietary Fiber: 1g
- Protein: 27.7g
- Total Sugars: 3g
- Potassium: 567mg

**PREPARATION: 20 MIN**

**COOKING: 20 MIN**

**SERVES: 8**

# 69. GARLIC PARMESAN CHICKEN WINGS

## INGREDIENTS

- Cooking spray
- ½ cup all-purpose flour
- Pepper to taste
- 2 tablespoons garlic powder
- 3 eggs, beaten
- 1¼ cups Parmesan cheese, grated
- 2 cups breadcrumbs
- 2 lb. chicken wings

## DIRECTIONS

1. Preheat your oven to 450 degrees F.
2. Spray baking pan with oil.
3. In a bowl, mix the flour, pepper and garlic powder.
4. Add eggs to another bowl.
5. Mix the Parmesan cheese and breadcrumbs in another bowl.
6. Dip the chicken wings in the first, second and third bowls.
7. Spray chicken wings with oil.
8. Bake in the oven for 20 minutes.

## NUTRITION

- Calories: 221
- Total Fat: 11.6g
- Saturated Fat: 3.9g
- Cholesterol: 122mg
- Sodium: 242mg
- Total Carbohydrate: 8g
- Dietary Fiber: 0.4g
- Protein: 16g
- Total Sugars: 3g
- Potassium: 163mg

**PREPARATION: 15 MIN**

**COOKING: 10 MIN**

**SERVES: 4**

# 70. CRISPY BAKED SHRIMP

## INGREDIENTS

- ¼ cup whole-wheat breadcrumbs
- 3 tablespoons olive oil, divided
- 1 ½ lb. jumbo shrimp, peeled and deveined
- Salt and pepper to taste
- 2 tablespoons lemon juice
- 1 tablespoon garlic, chopped
- 2 tablespoons butter
- ¼ cup Parmesan cheese, grated
- 2 tablespoons chives, chopped

## DIRECTIONS

1. Preheat your oven to 425 degrees F.
2. Add breadcrumbs to a pan over medium heat.
3. Cook until toasted.
4. Transfer to a plate.
5. Coat baking pan with 1 tablespoon oil.
6. Arrange shrimp in a single layer in a baking pan.
7. Season with salt and pepper.
8. Mix lemon juice, garlic and butter in a bowl.
9. Pour mixture on top of the shrimp.
10. Add Parmesan cheese and chives to the breadcrumbs.
11. Sprinkle breadcrumbs on top of the shrimp.
12. Bake for 10 minutes.

## NUTRITION

- Calories: 340
- Total Fat: 18.7g
- Saturated Fat: 6g
- Cholesterol: 293mg
- Sodium: 374mg
- Total Carbohydrate: 6g
- Dietary Fiber: 0.8g
- Protein: 36.9g
- Total Sugars: 2g
- Potassium: 483mg

**PREPARATION: 20 MIN**

**COOKING: 1 HOUR**

**SERVES: 6**

# 71. HERBED MEDITERRANEAN FISH FILLET

## INGREDIENTS

- 3 lb. sea bass fillet
- Salt to taste
- 2 tablespoons tarragon, chopped
- ¼ cup dry white wine
- 3 tablespoons olive oil, divided
- 1 tablespoon butter
- 2 garlic cloves, minced
- 2 cups whole-wheat breadcrumbs
- 3 tablespoons parsley, chopped
- 3 tablespoons oregano, chopped
- 3 tablespoons fresh basil, chopped

## DIRECTIONS

1. Preheat your oven to 350 degrees F.
2. Season fish with salt and tarragon.
3. Pour half of oil into a roasting pan.
4. Stir in wine.
5. Add the fish in the roasting pan.
6. Bake in the oven for 50 minutes.
7. Add remaining oil to a pan over medium heat.
8. Cook herbs, breadcrumbs and salt.
9. Spread breadcrumb mixture on top of fish and bake for 5 minutes.

## NUTRITION

- Calories: 288
- Total Fat: 12.7g
- Saturated Fat: 2.9g
- Cholesterol: 65mg
- Sodium: 499mg
- Total Carbohydrate: 10.4g
- Dietary Fiber: 1.8g
- Protein: 29.5g
- Total Sugars: 1g
- Potassium: 401 mg

**PREPARATION: 10 MIN**

**COOKING: 10 MIN**

**SERVES: 4**

# 72. MUSHROOM STUFFED WITH RICOTTA

## INGREDIENTS

- 4 large mushrooms, stemmed
- 1 tablespoon olive oil
- Salt and pepper to taste
- ¼ cup basil, chopped
- 1 cup ricotta cheese
- ¼ cup Parmesan cheese, grated

## DIRECTIONS

1. Preheat your grill.
2. Coat the mushrooms with oil.
3. Season with salt and pepper.
4. Grill for 5 minutes.
5. Stuff each mushroom with a mixture of basil, ricotta cheese and Parmesan cheese.
6. Grill for another 5 minutes.

## NUTRITION

- Calories: 259
- Total Fat: 17.3g
- Saturated Fat: 5.4g
- Cholesterol: 24mg
- Sodium: 509mg
- Total Carbohydrate: 14.9g
- Dietary Fiber: 2.6g
- Protein: 12.2g
- Total Sugars: 7g
- Potassium: 572mg

**PREPARATION: 15 MIN**

**COOKING: 0 MIN**

**SERVES: 4**

# 73. THAI CHOPPED SALAD

## INGREDIENTS

- 10 oz. kale and cabbage mix
- 14 oz. tofu, sliced into cubes and fried crispy
- ½ cup vinaigrette

## DIRECTIONS

1. Arrange kale and cabbage in a serving platter.
2. Top with the tofu cubes.
3. Drizzle with the vinaigrette.

## NUTRITION

- Calories: 332
- Total Fat: 15g
- Saturated Fat: 1.5g
- Cholesterol: 0mg
- Sodium: 236mg
- Total Carbohydrate: 26.3g
- Dietary Fiber: 7.6g
- Protein: 1.3g
- Total Sugars: 13g
- Potassium: 41mg

**PREPARATION: 10 MIN**

**COOKING: 15 MIN**

**SERVES: 4**

# 74. LEMON & ROSEMARY SALMON

## INGREDIENTS

- 4 salmon fillets
- Salt and pepper to taste
- 4 tablespoons butter
- 1 lemon, sliced
- 8 rosemary sprigs

## DIRECTIONS

1. Season salmon with salt and pepper.
2. Place salmon on a foil sheet.
3. Top with butter, lemon slices and rosemary sprigs.
4. Fold the foil and seal.
5. Bake in the oven at 450 degrees F for 15 minutes.

## NUTRITION

- Calories: 365
- Total Fat: 22g
- Saturated Fat: 6g
- Cholesterol: 86mg
- Sodium: 445mg
- Total Carbohydrate: 5g
- Dietary Fiber: 1.9g
- Protein: 29.8g
- Total Sugars: 3g
- Potassium: 782mg

**PREPARATION: 20 MIN**　　**COOKING: 25 MIN**　　**SERVES: 6**

# 75. CHICKEN KURMA

## INGREDIENTS

- 1 tablespoon olive oil
- 1 onion, diced
- 3 garlic cloves, sliced thinly
- 1 ginger, minced
- 2 tomatoes, diced
- 1 serrano pepper, minced
- Salt and pepper to taste
- 1 teaspoon ground turmeric
- 1 tablespoon tomato paste
- 1 ½ lb. chicken, sliced
- 1 red bell pepper, chopped

## DIRECTIONS

1. Pour oil into a pan over medium heat.
2. Cook onion for 3 minutes.
3. Add garlic, ginger, tomatoes, Serrano pepper, salt, pepper, and turmeric and tomato paste.
4. Bring to a boil.
5. Reduce heat and simmer for 10 minutes.
6. Add chicken and cook for 5 minutes.
7. Stir in red bell pepper.
8. Cook for 5 minutes.

## NUTRITION

- Calories: 175
- Total Fat: 15.2g
- Saturated Fat: 3g
- Cholesterol: 115mg

- Sodium: 400mg
- Total Carbohydrate: 7g
- Dietary Fiber: 1.8g
- Protein: 24g

- Total Sugars: 3g
- Potassium: 436mg

**PREPARATION: 20 MIN**

**COOKING: 25 MIN**

**SERVES: 4**

# 76. BAKED LEMON & PEPPER CHICKEN

## INGREDIENTS

- 4 chicken breast fillets
- Salt to taste
- 1 tablespoon olive oil
- 1 lemon, sliced thinly
- 1 tablespoon maple syrup
- 2 tablespoons lemon juice
- 2 tablespoons butter
- Pepper to taste

## DIRECTIONS

1. Preheat your oven to 425 degrees F.
2. Season chicken with salt.
3. Pour oil into a pan over medium heat.
4. Cook chicken for 5 minutes per side.
5. Transfer chicken to a baking pan.
6. Surround the chicken with the lemon slices.
7. Bake in the oven for 10 minutes.
8. Pour in maple syrup and lemon juice to the pan.
9. Put the butter on top of the chicken.
10. Sprinkle with pepper.
11. Bake for another 5 minutes.

## NUTRITION

- Calories: 286
- Total Fat: 13g
- Saturated Fat: 5g
- Cholesterol: 109mg
- Sodium: 448mg
- Total Carbohydrate: 7g
- Dietary Fiber: 1.4g
- Protein: 34.8g
- Total Sugars: 3g
- Potassium: 350mg

**PREPARATION: 5 MIN**

**COOKING: 30 MIN**

**SERVES: 4**

# 77. SKILLET CHICKEN WITH WHITE WINE SAUCE

## INGREDIENTS

- 4 boneless chicken thighs
- 1 tsp. garlic powder
- 1 tsp. dried thyme
- 1 tbsp. olive oil
- 1 tbsp. butter
- 1 yellow onion diced
- 3 garlic cloves minced
- 1 cup dry white wine
- ½ cup heavy cream
- Fresh chopped parsley
- Salt and pepper

## DIRECTIONS

1. Heat your oil in a skillet. Season your chicken, add it to the skillet, and then cook it about 5-7 mins.
2. Flip the chicken and cook until looking golden brown.
3. Remove the chicken to a plate.
4. Add butter to the skillet. Then add onions and cook them until softened.
5. Stir in garlic salt and pepper, add wine and cook for 4-5 mins.
6. Stir in the thyme and the heavy cream.
7. Place the breasts back to the skillet and leave to simmer for 2-3 mins. Top them with the parsley.

## NUTRITION

- Calories: 276kcal
- Fats: 21g
- Carbs: 6g

- Protein: 25g

**PREPARATION: 10 MIN**

**COOKING: 18 MIN**

**SERVES: 3**

# 78. STIR FRY KIMCHI AND PORK BELLY

## INGREDIENTS

- 300g pork belly
- 1 lb. kimchi
- 1 tbsp. soy sauce
- 1 tbsp. rice wine
- 1 tbsp. sesame seeds
- 1 stalk green onion

## DIRECTIONS

1. Slice the pork as thin as possible and marinate it in soy sauce and rice wine for 8-10 mins.
2. Heat a pan. When very hot, add the pork belly and stir-fry until brown.
3. Add the kimchi to the pan and stir-fry for 2 mins to let the flavors completely mix.
4. Turn off heat and slice the green onion. Top with sesame seeds.

## NUTRITION

- Calories: 790 kcal
- Fats: 68g
- Carbs: 7g

- Protein: 14g

**PREPARATION: 10 MIN**

**COOKING: 10 MIN**

**SERVES: 2**

# 79. LEMON BUTTER SAUCE WITH FISH

## INGREDIENTS

- 150g thin white fish fillets
- 4 tbsps. butter
- 2 tbsps. white flour
- 2 tbsps. olive oil
- 1 tbsp. fresh lemon juice
- Salt and pepper
- Chopped parsley

## DIRECTIONS

1. Place the butter in a small skillet over medium heat. Melt it and leave it, just stirring it casually. After 3 mins, pour into a small bowl.
2. Add lemon juice and season it and set it aside.
3. Dry the fish with paper towels, season it to taste, and sprinkle with flour.
4. Heat oil in a skillet over high heat: when shimmering, add the fish and cook around 2-3 mins.
5. Remove to a plate and serve with the sauce. Top with parsley.

## NUTRITION

- Calories: 371 kcal
- Fats: 27g
- Carbs: 3g
- Protein: 30g

**PREPARATION: 5 MIN**

**COOKING: 25 MIN**

**SERVES: 8**

# 80. PRESSURE COOKER CRACK CHICKEN

## INGREDIENTS

- 2 lbs. boneless chicken thighs.
- 2 slices bacon
- 8 ozs. cream cheese
- 1 scallion sliced
- ½ cup shredded cheddar
- 1 ½ tsp. garlic and onion powder
- 1 tsp. red pepper flakes and dried dill
- Salt and pepper
- 2 tbsps. apple cider vinegar
- 1 tbsp. dried chives

## DIRECTIONS

1. On pressure cooker, use sauté mode and wait for it to heat up. Add the bacon and cook until crispy. Then set aside on a plate.
2. Add everything in the pot, except the cheddar cheese. On Manual high, pressure cook them for 15 mins and then release it.
3. On a large plate, shred the chicken and then return to the pot and the cheddar.
4. Top with the bacon and scallion.

## NUTRITION

- Calories: 437kcal
- Fats: 28g
- Carbs: 5g
- Protein: 41g

**PREPARATION: 10 MIN**

**COOKING: 90-120 MIN**

**SERVES: 3**

# 81. BACON BLEU CHEESE FILLED EGGS

## INGREDIENTS

- 8 eggs
- ¼ cup crumbled bleu cheese
- 3 slices of cooked bacon
- ¼ cup sour cream
- 1/3 cup mayo
- ¼ tsp. pepper and dill
- ½ tsp. salt
- 1 tbsp. mustard
- Parsley

## DIRECTIONS

1. Hard boil your eggs and then cut them half. Place the yolks in a bowl.
2. With a fork, mash the yolks, add the sour cream, mayo, bleu cheese, mustard, and the seasoning and mix until creamy enough for your taste. Slice up the bacon to small pieces. Stir in the rest of the ingredients and fill up the eggs.

## NUTRITION

- Calories: 217kcal
- Fats: 16g
- Carbs: 1g

- Protein: 6g

# 82. SPINACH STUFFED CHICKEN BREASTS

## INGREDIENTS

- 1 ½ lbs. chicken breasts
- 4 ozs. cream cheese
- ¼ cup frozen spinach
- ½ cup mozzarella
- 4 oz. artichoke hearts
- ¼ cup Greek yogurt
- Salt and pepper
- 2 tbsps. olive oil

## DIRECTIONS

1. Pound the breasts about 1 inch thick. Cut each chicken down the middle, but don't cut through it. Make a pocket for the filling: season the chicken.
2. In a bowl, combine the Greek yogurt, mozzarella, cream cheese, artichoke, and spinach. Next, season it. Mix until well-combined.
3. Fill all breasts equally with your mixture.
4. In a skillet over medium heat, add the oil and place your chicken. Cover the skillet and cook for 5-6 mins, turning the heat up in the last 1-2 mins.

## NUTRITION

- Calories: 288 kcal
- Fats: 18g
- Carbs: 3g

- Protein: 31g

**PREPARATION: 5 MIN**

**COOKING: 20 MIN**

**SERVES: 4**

# 83. CHICKEN WITH LEMON AND GARLIC

## INGREDIENTS

- 4 boneless chicken thighs
- 2 garlic cloves minced
- Juice of 1 lemon
- ¼ tsp. smoked paprika, red chili flakes, garlic powder
- 2 tsps. Italian seasoning
- 1 tbsp. heavy cream
- Fresh parsley
- ¼ small onion
- 1 tbsp. olive oil
- 1½ tbsp. butter
- Salt and pepper

## DIRECTIONS

1. Season your chicken with all spices.
2. In a skillet over medium heat, add the olive oil and cook for 5-6 mins on each side. Set aside on a plate.
3. Heat the skillet again and add in the butter. Stir in onion and garlic and add your lemon juice. Season them with everything left. After that, stir in your heavy cream. Once the sauce has thickened up, add the chicken back to the pot.
4. Serve it with lemon slices.

## NUTRITION

- Calories: 279kcal
- Fats: 15g
- Carbs: 3g
- Protein: 15g

**PREPARATION: 3H**

**COOKING: 35 MIN**

**SERVES: 6**

# 84. CHICKEN POT PIE IN A SLOW COOKER

## INGREDIENTS

**For the filling:**
- 1 cup chicken broth
- ¾ cup heavy whipping cream
- 3 ½ oz. cooked chicken
- ½ cup mixed veggies
- ¼ onion
- 2garlic cloves
- salt and pepper
- ¼ tsp. rosemary
- 1 tsp. poultry seasoning

**For the crust:**
- 4 eggs
- 4 ½ tbsps. butter
- 1/3 cup coconut flour
- 1 1/3 cup shredded cheddar
- 2 tsps. full-fat sour cream
- ¼ tsp. baking powder

## DIRECTIONS

1. Cook 1-1 ½ lbs. chicken in the slow cooker for 3 hours on high.
2. Preheat your oven to 400°F.
3. Sauté your onion, veggies, garlic cloves and season with 2 tbsp. butter in a skillet for 5-6 mins.
4. Add in the whipping cream, chicken broth, poultry, thyme, and rosemary.
5. Simmer them covered for 5 mins and don't forget to use a lot of liquid; otherwise, it will be really dry. Add the diced chicken, too.
6. Make the breading by mixing melted butter, salt, sour cream, and eggs before whisking them.
7. Add coconut flour and baking powder and stir until well-combined.
8. Stir in the cheddar cheese.
9. Bake in a 400°F oven for 15-20 mins.
10. Set oven to broil and move the pie to the top shelf. Broil for 2-4 mins to brown nicely.

## NUTRITION

- Calories: 301 kcal
- Carbs: 5g
- Protein: 15g

- Fats: 24g

**PREPARATION: 10 MIN**

**COOKING: 35 MIN**

**SERVES: 6**

# 85. CHEESE CAULI BREADSTICKS

## INGREDIENTS

- 4 eggs
- 4 cups cauli
- 3 cups mozzarella cheese
- 4 garlic cloves
- 3 tsps. oregano
- Salt and pepper

## DIRECTIONS

1. Preheat your oven 425°F. Prepare one baking sheet with paper on it.
2. Chop your cauli to florets. Add them to a food processor and then pulse.
3. Microwave it for 10 mins and then let it cool afterward. In a large bowl, add in the cauli, eggs, 2 cups of cheese, oregano, garlic and season it, while mixing it.
4. Place the mixture on your sheet while forming your desired shape. Bake it for 20-25 mins. Finally, top it with the rest of the cheese and bake for another 5 mins until golden and well melted.

## NUTRITION

- Calories: 185kcal
- Carbs: 4g
- Protein: 11g
- Fats: 12g

# 86. MOZZARELLA CAULIFLOWER BARS

## INGREDIENTS

- 1 big cauliflower head, riced
- ½ cup low-fat mozzarella cheese, shredded
- ¼ cup egg whites
- 1 teaspoon Italian seasoning
- Black pepper to the taste

## DIRECTIONS

1. Spread the cauliflower rice on a lined baking sheet, cook in the oven at 375 degrees F for 20 minutes, transfer to a bowl, add black pepper, cheese, seasoning and egg whites, stir well, spread into a rectangle pan and press well on the bottom.
2. Introduce in the oven at 375 degrees F, bake for 20 minutes, cut into 12 bars and serve as a snack.

## NUTRITION

- Calories: 140
- Fat: 1g
- Fiber: 3g

- Carbs: 6g
- Protein: 6g

**PREPARATION: 10 MIN**

**COOKING: 40 MIN**

**SERVES: 4**

# 87. SHRIMP AND PINEAPPLE SALSA

## INGREDIENTS

- 1-pound large shrimp, peeled and deveined
- 20 ounces canned pineapple chunks
- 1 tablespoon garlic powder
- 1 cup red bell peppers, chopped
- Black pepper to the taste

## DIRECTIONS

1. Place shrimp in a baking dish, add pineapple, garlic, bell peppers and black pepper, toss a bit, introduce in the oven, bake at 375 degrees F for 40 minutes, divide into small bowls and serve cold.

## NUTRITION

- Calories: 170
- Fat: 5g
- Fiber: 4g
- Carbs: 15g
- Protein: 11g

# 88. STRAWBERRY BUCKWHEAT PANCAKES

## INGREDIENTS

- 100g (3½oz) strawberries, chopped
- 100g (3½ oz.) buckwheat flour
- 1 egg
- 250mls (8fl oz.) milk
- 1 teaspoon olive oil
- 1 teaspoon olive oil for frying
- Freshly squeezed juice of 1 orange
- 175 calories per serving

## DIRECTIONS

1. Pour the milk into a bowl and mix in the egg and a teaspoon of olive oil. Sift in the flour to the liquid mixture until smooth and creamy. Allow it to rest for 15 minutes. Heat a little oil in a pan and pour in a quarter of the mixture (or to the size you prefer.) Sprinkle in a quarter of the strawberries into the batter. Cook for around 2 minutes on each side. Serve hot with a drizzle of orange juice. You could try experimenting with other berries such as blueberries and blackberries

## NUTRITION

- Calories: 175
- Fat: 7g
- Fiber: 4g
- Carbs: 18g
- Protein: 5g

**PREPARATION: 10 MIN**

**COOKING: 50 MIN**

**SERVES: 12**

# 89. STRAWBERRY & NUT GRANOLA

## INGREDIENTS

- 200g (7oz) oats
- 250g (9oz) buckwheat flakes
- 100g (3½ oz.) walnuts, chopped
- 100g (3½ oz.) almonds, chopped
- 100g (3½ oz.) dried strawberries
- 1½ teaspoons ground ginger
- 1½ teaspoons ground cinnamon
- 120mls (4fl oz.) olive oil
- 2 tablespoon honey

## DIRECTIONS

1. Combine the oats, buckwheat flakes, nuts, ginger and cinnamon. In a saucepan, warm the oil and honey. Stir until the honey has melted. Pour the warm oil into the dry ingredients and mix well. Spread the mixture out on a large baking tray (or two) and bake in the oven at 150°C (300°F) for around 50 minutes until the granola is golden. Allow it to cool. Add in the dried berries. Store in an airtight container until ready to use. Can be served with yogurt, milk or even dry as a handy snack.

## NUTRITION

- Calories: 391
- Fat: 0g
- Fiber: 6g
- Carbs: 3g
- Protein: 8g

# 90. CHILLED STRAWBERRY & WALNUT PORRIDGE

## INGREDIENTS

- 100g (3½ oz.) strawberries
- 50g (2oz) rolled oats
- 4 walnut halves, chopped
- 1 teaspoon chia seeds
- 200mls (7fl oz.) unsweetened soya milk
- 100ml (3½ FL oz.) water

## DIRECTIONS

1. Place the strawberries, oats, soya milk and water into a blender and process until smooth. Stir in the chia seeds and mix well. Chill in the fridge overnight and serve in the morning with a sprinkling of chopped walnuts. It's simple and delicious.

## NUTRITION

- Calories: 384
- Fat: 2g
- Fiber: 5g
- Carbs: 3g
- Protein: 7g

**PREPARATION: 5 MIN**

**COOKING: 0 MIN**

**SERVES: 1**

# 91. FRUIT & NUT YOGURT CRUNCH

## INGREDIENTS

- 100g (3½ oz.) plain Greek yogurt
- 50g (2oz) strawberries, chopped
- 6 walnut halves, chopped
- Sprinkling of cocoa powder

## DIRECTIONS

1. Stir half of the chopped strawberries into the yogurt. Using a glass, place a layer of yogurt with a sprinkling of strawberries and walnuts, followed by another layer of the same until you reach the top of the glass. Garnish with walnuts pieces and a dusting of cocoa powder.

## NUTRITION

- Calories: 296
- Fat: 4g
- Fiber: 2g

- Carbs: 5g
- Protein: 9g

**PREPARATION: 5 MIN**

**COOKING: 15 MIN**

**SERVES: 4**

# 92. CHEESY BAKED EGGS

## INGREDIENTS

- 4 large eggs
- 75g (3oz) cheese, grated
- 25g (1oz) fresh rocket (arugula) leaves, finely chopped
- 1 tablespoon parsley
- ½ teaspoon ground turmeric
- 1 tablespoon olive oil

## DIRECTIONS

1. Grease each ramekin dish with a little olive oil. Divide the rocket (arugula) between the ramekin dishes then break an egg into each one. Sprinkle a little parsley and turmeric on top then sprinkle on the cheese. Place the ramekins in a preheated oven at 220°C/425°F for 15 minutes, until the eggs are set and the cheese is bubbling.

## NUTRITION

- Calories: 198
- Fat: 9g
- Fiber: 3g

- Carbs: 2g
- Protein: 13g

**PREPARATION: 10 MIN**

**COOKING: 5 MIN**

**SERVES: 1**

# 93. GREEN EGG SCRAMBLE

## INGREDIENTS

- 2 eggs, whisked
- 25g (1oz) rocket (arugula) leaves
- 1 teaspoon chives, chopped
- 1 teaspoon fresh basil, chopped
- 1 teaspoon fresh parsley, chopped
- 1 tablespoon olive oil

## DIRECTIONS

1. Mix the eggs together with the rocket (arugula) and herbs. Heat the oil in a frying pan and pour into the egg mixture. Gently stir until it's lightly scrambled. Season and serve.

## NUTRITION

- Calories: 250
- Fat: 5g
- Fiber: 7g
- Carbs: 8g
- Protein: 11g

**PREPARATION: 10 MIN**

**COOKING: 5 MIN**

**SERVES: 1**

# 94. SPICED SCRAMBLE

## INGREDIENTS

- 25g (1oz) kale, finely chopped
- 2 eggs
- 1 spring onion (scallion) finely chopped
- 1 teaspoon turmeric
- 1 tablespoon olive oil
- Sea salt
- Freshly ground black pepper

## DIRECTIONS

1. Crack the eggs into a bowl. Add the turmeric and whisk them. Season with salt and pepper. Heat the oil in a frying pan, add the kale and spring onions (scallions) and cook until it has wilted. Pour in the beaten eggs and stir until eggs have scrambled together with the kale.

## NUTRITION

- Calories: 259
- Fat: 3g
- Fiber: 4g
- Carbs: 3g
- Protein: 9g

**PREPARATION: 10 MIN**

**COOKING: 20 MIN**

**SERVES: 3**

# 95. POTATO BITES

## INGREDIENTS

- 1 potato, sliced
- 2 bacon slices, already cooked and crumbled
- 1 small avocado, pitted and cubed
- Cooking spray

## DIRECTIONS

1. Spread potato slices on a lined baking sheet, spray with cooking oil, introduce in the oven at 350 degrees F, bake for 20 minutes, arrange on a platter, top each slice with avocado and crumbled bacon and serve as a snack.

## NUTRITION

- Calories: 180
- Fat: 4g
- Fiber: 1g

- Carbs: 8g
- Protein: 6g

**PREPARATION: 10 MIN**

**COOKING: 10 MIN**

**SERVES: 4**

# 96. EGGPLANT SALSA

## INGREDIENTS

- 1 and ½ cups tomatoes, chopped
- 3 cups eggplant, cubed
- A drizzle of olive oil
- 2 teaspoons capers
- 6 ounces green olives, pitted and sliced
- 4 garlic cloves, minced
- 2 teaspoons balsamic vinegar
- 1 tablespoon basil, chopped
- Black pepper to the taste

## DIRECTIONS

1. Heat a saucepan with the oil medium-high heat, add eggplant, stir and cook for 5 minutes.
2. Add tomatoes, capers, olives, garlic, vinegar, basil and black pepper, toss, cook for 5 minutes more, divide into small cups and serve cold.

## NUTRITION

- Calories: 120
- Fat: 6g
- Fiber: 5g
- Carbs: 9g
- Protein: 7g

# 97. CARROTS AND CAULIFLOWER SPREAD

## INGREDIENTS

- 1 cup carrots, sliced
- 2 cups cauliflower florets
- ½ cup cashews
- 2 and ½ cups water
- 1 cup almond milk
- 1 teaspoon garlic powder
- ¼ teaspoon smoked paprika

## DIRECTIONS

1. In a small pot, mix the carrots with cauliflower, cashews and water, stir, cover, bring to a boil over medium heat, cook for 40 minutes, drain and transfer to a blender.
2. Add almond milk, garlic powder and paprika, pulse well, divide into small bowls and serve

## NUTRITION

- Calories: 201
- Fat: 7g
- Fiber: 4g

- Carbs: 7g
- Protein: 7g

**PREPARATION: 10 MIN**

**COOKING: 0 MIN**

**SERVES: 6**

# 98. BLACK BEAN SALSA

## INGREDIENTS

- 1 tablespoon coconut aminos
- ½ teaspoon cumin, ground
- 1 cup canned black beans, no-salt-added, drained and rinsed
- 1 cup salsa
- 6 cups romaine lettuce leaves, torn
- ½ cup avocado, peeled, pitted and cubed

## DIRECTIONS

1. In a bowl, combine the beans with the aminos, cumin, salsa, lettuce and avocado, toss, divide into small bowls and serve as a snack.

## NUTRITION

- Calories: 181
- Fat: 4g
- Fiber: 7g
- Carbs: 14g
- Protein: 7g

**PREPARATION: 10 MIN**

**COOKING: 0 MIN**

**SERVES: 2**

# 99. MUNG SPROUTS SALSA

## INGREDIENTS

- 1 red onion, chopped
- 2 cups Mung beans, sprouted
- A pinch of red chili powder
- 1 green chili pepper, chopped
- 1 tomato, chopped
- 1 teaspoon chaat masala
- 1 teaspoon lemon juice
- 1 tablespoon coriander, chopped
- Black pepper to the taste

## DIRECTIONS

1. In a salad bowl, mix onion with Mung sprouts, chili pepper, tomato, chili powder, chaat masala, lemon juice, coriander and pepper, toss well, divide into small cups and serve.

## NUTRITION

- Calories: 100
- Fiber: 1g
- Fat: 3g
- Carbs: 3g
- Protein: 6g

**PREPARATION: 10 MIN**

**COOKING: 0 MIN**

**SERVES: 4**

# 100. SPROUTS AND APPLES SNACK SALAD

## INGREDIENTS

- 1-pound Brussels sprouts, shredded
- 1 cup walnuts, chopped
- 1 apple, cored and cubed
- 1 red onion, chopped

**For the salad dressing:**
- 3 tablespoons red vinegar
- 1 tablespoon mustard
- ½ cup olive oil
- 1 garlic clove, minced
- Black pepper to the taste

## DIRECTIONS

1. In a salad bowl, mix sprouts with apple, onion and walnuts.
2. In another bowl, mix vinegar with mustard, oil, garlic and pepper, whisk really well, add this to your salad, toss well and serve as a snack.

## NUTRITION

- Calories: 120
- Fat: 2g
- Fiber: 2g
- Carbs: 8g
- Protein: 6g

**PREPARATION: 10 MIN**

**COOKING: 0 MIN**

**SERVES: 4**

# 101. DIJON CELERY SALAD

## INGREDIENTS

- 5 teaspoons stevia
- ½ cup lemon juice
- 1/3 cup Dijon mustard
- 2/3 cup olive oil
- Black pepper to the taste
- 2 apples, cored, peeled and cubed
- 1 bunch celery and leaves, roughly chopped
- ¾ cup walnuts, chopped

## DIRECTIONS

1. In a salad bowl, mix celery and its leaves with apple pieces and walnuts.
2. Add black pepper, lemon juice, mustard, stevia and olive oil, whisk well, add to your salad, toss, divide into small cups and serve as a snack.

## NUTRITION

- Calories: 125
- Fat: 2g
- Fiber: 2g
- Carbs: 7g
- Protein: 7g

# 102. NAPA CABBAGE SLAW

## INGREDIENTS

- ½ cup of red bell pepper, cut into thin strips
- 1 carrot, grated
- 4 cups Napa cabbage, shredded
- 3 green onions, chopped
- 1 tablespoon olive oil
- 2 teaspoons ginger, grated
- ½ teaspoon red pepper flakes, crushed
- 3 tablespoons balsamic vinegar
- 1 tablespoon coconut aminos
- 3 tablespoons low-fat peanut butter

## DIRECTIONS

1. In a salad bowl, mix bell pepper with carrot, cabbage and onions and toss.
2. Add oil, ginger, pepper flakes, vinegar, aminos and peanut butter, toss, divide into small cups and serve.

## NUTRITION

- Calories: 160
- Fat: 10g
- Fiber: 3g
- Carbs: 10g
- Protein: 5g

**PREPARATION: 10 MIN**

**COOKING: 0 MIN**

**SERVES: 4**

# 103. DILL BELL PEPPER BOWLS

## INGREDIENTS

- 2 tablespoons dill, chopped
- 1 yellow onion, chopped
- 1 pound multi colored bell peppers, cut into halves, seeded and cut into thin strips
- 3 tablespoons olive oil
- 2 and ½ tablespoons white vinegar
- Black pepper to the taste

## DIRECTIONS

1. In a salad bowl, mix bell peppers with onion, dill, pepper, oil and vinegar, toss to coat, divide into small bowls and serve as a snack.

## NUTRITION

- Calories: 120
- Fat: 3g
- Fiber: 4g
- Carbs: 2g
- Protein: 3g

# 12. VEGETABLES

# 104. BOK CHOY STIR FRY WITH FRIED BACON SLICES

## INGREDIENTS

- 2 cups Bok choy; chopped
- 2 Garlic cloves; minced
- 2 Bacon slices; chopped
- A drizzle of avocado oil
- Salt and black pepper to the taste.

## DIRECTIONS

1. Take a pan and heat it with oil over medium heat.
2. When the oil is hot, add bacon and keep stirring it until it's brown and crispy.
3. Transfer them to paper towels to drain out the excess oil.
4. Now bring the pan to medium heat and in it add garlic and bok choy.
5. Again give it a stir and cook it for 5 minutes.
6. Now drizzle and add some salt, pepper and the fried bacon and stir them for another 1 minute.
7. Turn off the heat and divide them in plates to serve.

## NUTRITION

- Calories: 50
- Fat: 1g
- Fiber: 1g

- Carbs: 2g
- Protein: 2g

**PREPARATION: 25 MIN**

**COOKING: 15 MIN**

**SERVES: 6**

# 105. NUTRITIONAL MUSTARD GREENS AND SPINACH SOUP

## INGREDIENTS

- 5 cups Spinach; torn
- ½ teaspoon Fenugreek seeds
- 1 teaspoon Cumin seeds
- 1 tablespoon Jalapeno; chopped
- 5 cups Mustard greens; chopped
- 2 teaspoons Ghee
- ½ Paprika
- 1 tablespoon Avocado oil
- 1 teaspoon Coriander seeds
- 1 cup Yellow onion; chopped
- 1 tablespoon Garlic; minced
- 1 tablespoon Ginger; grated
- ½ teaspoon Turmeric; ground
- 3 cups Coconut milk
- Salt and black pepper to the taste

## DIRECTIONS

1. Add coriander, fenugreek and cumin seed in a heated pot with oil over medium high heat.
2. Now stir and brow them for 2 minutes.
3. In the same pot, add onions and again stir them for 3 minutes.
4. Now after the onion's cooked, add half of the garlic, jalapenos, ginger and turmeric.
5. Again, give it a good stir and cook for another 3 minutes.
6. Add some more mustard greens, spinach and saute everything for 10 minutes.
7. After it's done add milk, salt, pepper before blending the soup with an immersion blender.
8. Now take another pan and heat it up over medium heat with some ghee drizzled on it.
9. In it, add garlic, paprika, and give it a good stir before turning off the heat.
10. Bring the soup to heat over medium heat and transfer them into soup bowls.
11. Top it with some drizzles of ghee and paprika. Now it's ready to serve hot.

## NUTRITION

- Calories: 143
- Fat: 6g
- Fiber: 3g
- Carbs: 7g
- Protein: 7g

**PREPARATION: 25 MIN**

**COOKING: 15 MIN**

**SERVES: 5**

# 106. BROCCOLI-CAULIFLOWER STEW

## INGREDIENTS

- 2 Bacon slices, chopped
- 1 Cauliflower head, separated into florets
- 1 Broccoli head, separated into florets
- 2 tbsp. Butter
- 2 Garlic cloves, minced
- Salt
- Black pepper

## DIRECTIONS

1. Put a pan on medium heat and dissolve the butter and the garlic. Add the bacon slices to brown for 3 minutes all over.
2. Mix in broccoli and cauliflower florets to cook for 2 minutes.
3. Pour water over it and cover the lid and let cook for 10 minutes.
4. Season with pepper and salt and puree soup with a dipping blend.
5. Let boil slowly for some minutes on medium heat.
6. Serve into bowls.

## NUTRITION

- Calories: 128
- Carbs: 4g
- Protein: 6g
- Fiber: 7g
- Fats: 2g

# 107. TOMATO AND BROCCOLI SOUP

## INGREDIENTS

- A drizzle of olive oil
- 28 oz. Canned sugar-free tomatoes
- ¼ tsp. Crushed red pepper
- 1 Broccoli head, into florets
- 1 Small ginger, chopped
- 1 Onion, chopped
- 1 Garlic clove, minced
- 2 tsp. Coriander seeds
- Black pepper
- Salt

## DIRECTIONS

1. Boil water and salt in a pan on medium-high and add broccoli florets to steam for 2 minutes.
2. Remove and put in a bowl of ice water. Drain and set aside.
3. Heat pan and put in coriander seeds to toast for 4 minutes. Blend in a blender and set aside.
4. Pour olive oil in a pot and set to medium and add red pepper, salt, pepper and onions and cook for 7 minutes.
5. Mix in coriander seeds and garlic and let it cook for 3 minutes.
6. Pour in tomatoes and let simmer for 10 minutes.
7. Mix in broccoli and cook for 12 minutes.
8. Serve

## NUTRITION

- Calories: 152
- Carbs: 1g
- Protein: 9g

- Fiber: 8g
- Fats: 9g

**PREPARATION: 20 MIN**

**COOKING: 15 MIN**

**SERVES: 4**

# 108. SHERRY WATERCRESS BROTH

## INGREDIENTS

- ¼ cup Sherry
- 6 ½ cups Watercress
- 6 cups Chicken stock
- 2 tsp. Coconut aminos
- 3 Whisked egg whites
- 3 Shallots: chopped
- 2 tsp. Sesame seeds
- Salt and pepper

## DIRECTIONS

1. Pour the stock into the pot and add sherry, coconut amino, salt and pepper and mix. Boil on medium heat.
2. Mix in watercress, shallots, and whisked whites and let boil.
3. Serve sprinkled with sesame seeds.

## NUTRITION

- Calories: 73
- Carbs: 7g
- Protein: 9g
- Fiber: 2g
- Fats: 7g

# 109. BOK CHOY MUSHROOM SOUP

## INGREDIENTS

- 2 Bacon strips, chopped
- 3 cups Beef stock
- 1 bunch Bok choy, chopped
- 1 Onion, chopped
- 3 tbsp. Parmesan cheese, grated
- 3 tbsp. Coconut aminos
- 2 tbsp Worcestershire sauce
- ½ tbsp. Red pepper flakes
- 1½ cups Mushrooms, chopped
- Black Pepper
- Salt

## DIRECTIONS

1. Put bacon in a saucepan over medium-high heat to brown until crispy then remove to paper towels to drain.
2. To medium heat, add the mushrooms and onions in the pan and cook for 15 minutes.
3. Pour in the stock, pepper flakes, aminos, bok choy, Worcestershire sauce, salt and pepper and mix.
4. Cook until bok choy is tender.
5. Serve into bowls and sprinkle with Parmesan cheese and bacon

## NUTRITION

- Calories: 100
- Carbs: 1g
- Protein: 5g
- Fiber: 9g
- Fats: 5g

**PREPARATION: 17 MIN**

**COOKING: 15 MIN**

**SERVES: 2**

# 110. FRIED GARLICY BACON AND BOK CHOY BROTH

## INGREDIENTS

- 2 cups Bok choy, chopped
- A drizzle of avocado oil
- 2 Bacon slices, chopped
- 2 Garlic cloves, minced
- Black pepper
- Salt

## DIRECTIONS

1. Put bacon in a pan on medium heat and let crisp. Remove and let drain on paper towels.
2. Add bok choy and garlic to the pan and let cook for 4 minutes.
3. Season with pepper and salt and put the bacon back into the pan.
4. Let cook for 1 minute and serve.

## NUTRITION

- Calories: 116
- Carbs: 8g
- Protein: 3g
- Fiber: 8g
- Fats: 1g

**PREPARATION: 20 MIN**

**COOKING: 15 MIN**

**SERVES: 4**

# 111. HASH BROWNS WITH RADISH

## INGREDIENTS

- 1/3 c. Shredded Parmesan cheese
- ½ tsp. Garlic powder
- Salt
- 1 lb. Shredded radishes
- Black pepper
- ½ tsp Onion powder.
- 4 Medium eggs

## DIRECTIONS

1. Set a large mixing bowl in a working surface.
2. Combine the seasonings, radishes, eggs, onion, and parmesan cheese
3. Arrange the mixture in a well-lined baking tray.
4. Set the oven for 10 minutes at 375°F. Allow to bake
5. Enjoy while still hot

## NUTRITION

- Calories: 104
- Fat: 6g
- Fiber: 8g
- Carbs: 5g
- Protein: 6g

# 112. BAKED RADISHES

## INGREDIENTS

- 1 tbsp. Chopped chives
- 15 Sliced radishes
- Salt
- Vegetable oil cooking spray
- Black pepper

## DIRECTIONS

1. Line your baking sheet well then spray with the cooking spray
2. Set the sliced radishes on the baking tray then sprinkle with cooking oil
3. Add the seasonings then top with chives
4. Set the oven for 10 minutes at 375°F, allow to bake
5. Turn the radishes to bake for 10 minutes
6. Serve cold

## NUTRITION

- Calories: 63
- Fat: 8g
- Fiber: 3g
- Carbs: 6g
- Protein: 1g

# 113. CREAMED CHEDDAR RADISHES

## INGREDIENTS

- Black pepper
- 7 oz. Halved radishes
- 2 Bacon slices
- 1 tbsp. Chopped green onion
- 2 tbsps. Sour cream
- Cayenne pepper powder
- Salt
- 1 tbsp. Grated cheddar cheese

## DIRECTIONS

1. Set the radishes in a saucepan then add water.
2. Let it boil for 10 minutes over medium heat then drain the water
3. Set your pan over medium-high heat to cook the bacon to a crispy texture.
4. Drain the excess grease in a paper towel and reserve
5. Set the same pan again over medium heat then stir-fry the radishes for seven minutes
6. Stir in the seasonings, sour cream, and cayenne pepper powder for 7 minutes
7. Serve with crumbled bacon topped with cheddar cheese

## NUTRITION

- Calories: 319
- Fat: 25g
- Fiber: 3g
- Carbs: 8g
- Protein: 11g

**PREPARATION: 30 MIN**

**COOKING: 45 MIN**

**SERVES: 4**

# 114. TASTY RADISH SOUP

## INGREDIENTS

- 1 Chopped onion
- Salt
- 2 Chopped celery stalk
- 6 c. Chicken stock
- 3 tbsps. Coconut oil
- 2 bunches Quartered radishes
- Black pepper
- 6 Minced garlic cloves

## DIRECTIONS

1. Set the pan over medium heat and melt the oil
2. Stir in the celery, onion, and garlic to cook until soft, about 5 minutes
3. Stir in the stock, radishes, and seasonings.
4. Cover and simmer to boil for 15 minutes
5. Enjoy while still hot

## NUTRITION

- Calories: 131
- Fat: 12g
- Fiber: 8g
- Carbs: 4g
- Protein: 1g

**PREPARATION: 10 MIN**

**COOKING: 15 MIN**

**SERVES: 4**

# 115. COLESLAW AVOCADO SALAD

## INGREDIENTS

- 1 tbsp. White vinegar
- Salt
- 2 tbsps. Olive oil
- Black pepper
- ¼ tsp. Lemon stevia
- Juice from 2 limes
- 2 Mashed avocados
- ¼ c. Chopped onion
- ¼ c. Chopped cilantro

**For coleslaw mix**

- 1 tsp. Salt
- ¼ Small red cabbage
- ½ Shredded carrot
- ¼ c. Lemon juice
- ½ Small green cabbage
- ¼ c. Olive oil
- 1 tbsp. Stevia
- Zest of ½ lemon

## DIRECTIONS

1. Set the mixing bowl in place to make the coleslaw salad
2. Add the mashed avocado and onions to coat well
3. Combine the seasonings, lime juice, vinegar, stevia, and oil in another bowl.
4. Add the mixture to the salad, mix to coat evenly
5. Enjoy

## NUTRITION

- Calories: 481
- Fat: 42g
- Fiber: 12g
- Carbs: 26g
- Protein: 6g

**PREPARATION: 17 MIN**

**COOKING: 15 MIN**

**SERVES: 4**

# 116. MUSTARD EGG AND AVOCADO SALAD

## INGREDIENTS

- Salt
- ¼ c. Mayonnaise
- 4 Medium eggs
- 1 Sliced avocado
- 2 tsps. Mustard
- 4 c. Mixed lettuce leaves
- 1 tbsp. Chopped chives,
- Black pepper
- 2 Minced garlic cloves

## DIRECTIONS

1. Set the cooking pan over medium-high heat.
2. Add water, eggs, and salt then allow to boil for about 7minutes.
3. Once boiled, drain the liquid, let cool then chop them.
4. Set a salad bowl in position to mix lettuce eggs and avocado
5. Toss with garlic, seasonings, and chives to coat
6. Combine the seasonings, mustard, and mayonnaise in another bowl
7. Add to the salad, toss and serve.

## NUTRITION

- Calories: 278
- Fat: 16g
- Fiber: 7g
- Carbs: 13g
- Protein: 12g

# 117. CUCUMBER AVOCADO SALAD MIX

## INGREDIENTS

- Salt
- 1 Sliced cucumber
- 2 Chopped avocados
- 2 tbsps. Olive oil
- 1 Sliced onion
- ¼ c. Chopped cilantro
- 2 tbsps. Lemon juice
- Black pepper
- 1 lb. Halved cherry tomatoes

## DIRECTIONS

1. Stir together cucumber, tomatoes, avocado, and onion in a salad bowl
2. Add the seasonings, lemon juice, and oil. Mix to coat well.
3. Serve cold topped with cilantro

## NUTRITION

- Calories: 310
- Fat: 27g
- Fiber: 1g
- Carbs: 16g
- Protein: 8g

# 118. CREAMY AVOCADO SOUP

## INGREDIENTS

- 3 c. Chicken stock
- Black pepper
- 2 Chopped scallions
- Salt
- 2/3 c. Heavy cream
- 2 tbsps. Butter
- 2 Chopped avocados

## DIRECTIONS

1. Over a medium source of heat, set the saucepan and cook the scallions for 2 minutes
2. Stir in 2 ½ cups stock to simmer for 3 minutes
3. Set the blender in position to blend avocados, heavy cream, the remaining stock, and seasonings.
4. Return to a pan to cook for 2 minutes as you adjust the seasoning
5. Serve in soup bowls

## NUTRITION

- Calories: 335
- Fat: 32g
- Fiber: 9g
- Carbs: 13g
- Protein: 3g

**PREPARATION: 5 MIN**

**COOKING: 8 MIN**

**SERVES: 2**

# 119. BUTTER ASPARAGUS WITH CREAMY EGGS

## INGREDIENTS

- 4 oz. asparagus
- 2 eggs, blended
- 1 oz. grated parmesan cheese
- 1-ounce sour cream
- 2 tbsp. butter, unsalted

**Seasoning:**
- 1/3 tsp salt
- 1/8 tsp ground black pepper
- ¼ tsp cayenne pepper
- ½ tbsp. avocado oil

## DIRECTIONS

1. Take a medium skillet pan, place it over medium heat, add butter and when it melts, add blended eggs and then cook for 2 to 3 minutes until scrambled to the desired level; don't overcook.
2. Spoon the scrambled eggs into a food processor, add 1/8 tsp salt, cayenne pepper, sour cream and cheese and then pulse for 1 minute until smooth.
3. Return skillet pan over medium heat, add oil and when hot, add asparagus, season with black pepper and remaining salt, toss until mixed and cook for 3 minutes or more until roasted.
4. Distribute asparagus between two plates, add egg mixture, and then serve.

## NUTRITION

- Calories: 338
- Fats: 28.5g
- Protein: 14.4g
- Net Carb: 4.7g
- Fiber: 1.2g

# 120. SPINACH EGG MUFFINS

## INGREDIENTS

- ½ cups chopped spinach
- 1/8 tsp dried basil
- 1/8 tsp garlic powder
- 2 large eggs
- 3 tbsp. grated Parmesan cheese

**Seasoning:**
- ¼ tsp of sea salt
- 1/8 tsp ground black pepper

## DIRECTIONS

1. Turn on the oven, then set it to 400 degrees F, and let preheat.
2. Meanwhile, place eggs in a bowl, season with salt and black pepper and whisk until blended.
3. Add garlic and basil, whisk in mixed and then stir in spinach and cheese until combined.
4. Take two silicone muffin cups, grease them with reserved bacon greased, fill them evenly with prepared egg mixture and bake for 8 to 10 minutes until the top has nicely browned.
5. Serve.

## NUTRITION

- Calories: 55
- Fats: 3.5g
- Protein: 4.5g
- Net Carb: 0.4g
- Fiber: 0.2g

**PREPARATION: 10 MIN**

**COOKING: 10 MIN**

**SERVES: 2**

# 121. BROCCOLI AND EGG MUFFIN

## INGREDIENTS

- ¼ cup broccoli florets, steamed, chopped
- 2 tbsp. grated cheddar cheese
- 1/16 tsp dried thyme
- 1/16 tsp garlic powder
- 1 egg

**Seasoning:**

- ¼ tsp salt
- 1/8 tsp ground black pepper

## DIRECTIONS

1. Turn on the oven, then set it to 400 degrees F and let it preheat.
2. Meanwhile, take two silicone muffin cups, grease them with oil, and evenly fill them with broccoli and cheese.
3. Crack the egg in a bowl, add garlic powder, thyme, salt, and black pepper, whisk well, then evenly pour the mixture into muffin cups and bake for 8 to 10 minutes until done.
4. Serve.

## NUTRITION

- Calories: 76
- Fats: 5.1g
- Protein: 5.7g
- Net Carb: 1.2g
- Fiber: 0.7g

# 122. JALAPENO AND CHEESE EGG MUFFINS

## INGREDIENTS

- 1 jalapeno pepper, diced
- 2 tbsp. sliced green onions
- 2 tbsp. grated parmesan cheese
- 1 tsp all-purpose seasoning
- 2 eggs

**Seasoning:**

- 1/3 tsp salt
- ¼ tsp ground black pepper

## DIRECTIONS

1. Turn on the oven, then set it to 375 degrees F, and let it preheat.
2. Meanwhile, take two silicone muffin cups, grease with oil, and evenly fill them with cheese, jalapeno pepper, and green onion.
3. Crack eggs in a bowl, season with salt, black pepper, and all-purpose seasoning, whisk well, then evenly pour the mixture into muffin cups and bake for 15 to 20 minutes or until the top is slightly brown and muffins have puffed up.
4. Serve.

## NUTRITION

- Calories: 108
- Fats: 7.1g
- Protein: 8.9g

- Net Carb: 1.8g
- Fiber: 0.4g

**PREPARATION: 10 MIN**

**COOKING: 12 MIN**

**SERVES: 2**

# 123. CHEESY TOMATO AND OLIVE MUFFINS

## INGREDIENTS

- 4 1/3 tbsp. almond flour
- ½ tbsp. coconut flour
- 1/3 tbsp. chopped tomato
- 1/3 tbsp. sliced green olives
- 2 tbsp. sour cream

**Seasoning:**
- 1/8 tsp baking powder
- 2/3 tbsp. avocado oil
- 3 tbsp. grated parmesan cheese
- ½ of egg

## DIRECTIONS

1. Turn on the oven, then set it to 320 degrees F and let it preheat.
2. Meanwhile, take a medium bowl, place flours in it, and stir in the baking powder until mixed.
3. Add eggs along with sour cream and oil, whisk until blended and then fold in cheese, tomato, and olives until just mixed.
4. Take two silicone muffin cups, add the prepared batter in it evenly and then bake for 10 to 12 minutes until cooked but slightly moist in the middle.
5. When done, let muffin cools for 5 minutes, then take them out and serve.

## NUTRITION

- Calories: 256
- Fats: 23.5g
- Protein: 8.7g

- Net Carb: 1g
- Fiber: 1.8g

# 124. PUMPKIN BREAD

## INGREDIENTS

- 6 tbsp. coconut flour
- 1 tbsp. erythritol sweetener
- ¼ tsp vanilla extract, unsweetened
- 1 egg
- 2 tbsp. pumpkin puree

**Seasoning:**
- ¼ tsp baking powder
- ¼ tsp cinnamon
- 1 tbsp. chopped almonds
- 1 ½ tbsp. butter, unsalted, softened

## DIRECTIONS

1. Turn on the oven, then set it to 350 degrees F and let it preheat.
2. Meanwhile, take a medium bowl, place butter in it, whisk in sugar and egg until fluffy.
3. Add remaining ingredients except for almonds, whisk until incorporated and smooth batter comes together and then fold in almonds until just mixed
4. Take a mini loaf pan, add the prepared batter in it and then bake for 20 to 23 minutes until firm and top have turned nicely browned.
5. When done, let the bread cool for 5 minutes, take out the bread, cut it into slices, and then serve.

## NUTRITION

- Calories: 240
- Fats: 17.7g
- Protein: 9.4g

- Net Carb: 1g
- Fiber: 8.4g

**PREPARATION: 5 MIN**

**COOKING: 12 MIN**

**SERVES: 2**

# 125. BUTTERY BROCCOLI AND BACON

## INGREDIENTS

- 1 slice of turkey bacon
- 1 cup chopped broccoli florets
- 1/8 tsp garlic powder
- ¼ tsp Italian seasoning
- ¼ tbsp. unsalted butter

**Seasoning:**
- 1/8 tsp salt
- 1/8 tsp ground black pepper

## DIRECTIONS

1. Take a medium skillet pan, place it over high heat, add bacon slice and cook for 3 to 5 minutes until crispy.
2. Transfer bacon to a cutting board and then chop it into small pieces.
3. Reduce the heat to medium-low level, add broccoli florets into the pan, stir well into the bacon grease, add butter, then toss until mixed and cook for 5 minutes until tender.
4. Season the broccoli florets with salt, black pepper, and Italian seasoning, add chopped bacon, stir well and cook for 2 minutes until thoroughly heated.
5. Serve.

## NUTRITION

- Calories: 77
- Fats: 5g
- Protein: 5g

- Net Carb: 1g
- Fiber: 2g

# 126. BROCCOLI SALAD WITH BACON

## INGREDIENTS

- 1 cup broccoli florets, chopped
- 4 tbsp. whipped topping
- 2 tbsp. shredded cheddar cheese
- 3 slices of turkey bacon, cooked, chopped
- 1/3 tsp garlic powder

**Seasoning:**
- 1/8 tsp salt
- 1/8 tsp dried parsley

## DIRECTIONS

1. Take a medium bowl, place whipped topping in it, whisk in garlic powder and parsley, and then fold in broccoli florets.
2. Top with bacon and cheddar cheese and serve.

## NUTRITION

- Calories: 119
- Fats: 10g
- Protein: 3.5g

- Net Carb: 2g
- Fiber: 0.5g

# 127. ROASTED GREEN BEANS

## INGREDIENTS

- ½ pound green beans
- ½ cup grated parmesan cheese
- 3 tbsp. coconut oil
- ½ tsp garlic powder

**Seasoning:**
- 1/3 tsp salt
- 1/8 tsp ground black pepper

## DIRECTIONS

1. Turn on the oven, then set it to 425 degrees F, and let preheat.
2. Take a baking sheet, line green beans on it, and set aside until required.
3. Prepare the dressing, and for this, place remaining ingredients in a bowl, except for cheese and whisk until combined.
4. Drizzle the dressing over green beans, toss until well coated, and then bake for 20 minutes until green beans are tender-crisp.
5. Then sprinkle cheese on top of beans and continue roasting for 3 to 5 minutes or until cheese melts and nicely golden brown.
6. Serve.

## NUTRITION

- Calories: 119
- Fats: 9g
- Protein: 5g
- Net Carb: 4.5g
- Fiber: 3g

**PREPARATION: 5 MIN**

**COOKING: 12 MIN**

**SERVES: 2**

# 128. FRIED CAULIFLOWER AND EGG RICE

## INGREDIENTS

- 8-ounce cauliflower florets, riced
- 2 green onion, sliced
- 1 large egg, beaten
- 1 tbsp. soy sauce
- ½ tsp toasted sesame oil

**Seasoning:**
- 1 tbsp. coconut oil
- ½ tsp garlic powder

## DIRECTIONS

1. Take a large skillet pan, place it over medium-high heat, add coconut oil and riced cauliflower, and cook for 5 minutes until softened.
2. Then add green onions, stir well and cook for 3 minutes until onions are tender.
3. Season with salt, sprinkle garlic over cauliflower, cook for 1 minute until fragrant, then pour in the egg, stir well and cook for 2 minutes until the egg has scrambled to desire level, stirring continuously.
4. Drizzle with soy sauce and sesame oil and Serve.

## NUTRITION

- Calories: 57
- Fats: 4g
- Protein: 3g

- Net Carb: 1.7g
- Fiber: 0.5g

**PREPARATION: 5 MIN**

**COOKING: 10 MIN**

**SERVES: 2**

# 129. SPINACH ZUCCHINI BOATS

## INGREDIENTS

- 1 large zucchini
- ¾ cup spinach
- 1 ½ tbsp. whipped topping
- 3 tbsp. grated parmesan cheese
- ½ tsp garlic powder

**Seasoning:**

- ½ tsp salt
- ½ tsp ground black pepper

## DIRECTIONS

1. Turn on the oven, then set it to 350 degrees F, and let preheat.
2. Take a skillet pan, place it over medium heat, add spinach and cook for 5 to 7 minutes or until spinach leaves have wilted and their moisture has evaporated completely.
3. Sprinkle garlic powder, ¼ tsp each of salt and black pepper over spinach, add whipped topping and 2 tbsp. cheese and stir well until the cheese has melted, remove the pan from heat.
4. Cut off the top and bottom of zucchini, then cut it in half lengthwise and make a well by scooping out pulp along the center, leaving ½-inch shell.
5. Season zucchini with remaining salt and black pepper, place them on a baking sheet and roast for 5 minutes.
6. Then fill zucchini evenly with spinach mixture, top with remaining cheese and broil for 3 minutes until cheese has melted.
7. Serve.

## NUTRITION

- Calories: 86.5
- Fats: 6g
- Protein: 4g
- Net Carb: 3.5g
- Fiber: 0.5g

# 130. GREEN BEANS WITH HERBS

## INGREDIENTS

- 3 oz. green beans
- 2 slices of bacon, diced
- 3 tbsp. chopped parsley
- 3 tbsp. chopped cilantro
- 1 tbsp. avocado oil

**Seasoning:**
- ½ tsp garlic powder
- ¼ tsp salt

## DIRECTIONS

1. Place green beans in a medium heatproof bowl, cover with a plastic wrap, and then microwave for 3 to 4 minutes at high heat setting until tender.
2. Meanwhile, take a medium skillet pan, place it over medium heat and when hot, add bacon and cook for 3 to 4 minutes until crisp.
3. Season bacon with salt, sprinkle with garlic powder and cook for 30 seconds until fragrant, remove the pan from heat.
4. When green beans have steamed, drain them well, rinse under cold water, and then transfer to a bowl.
5. Add bacon and remaining ingredients and toss until well mixed.
6. Serve.

## NUTRITION

- Calories: 380
- Fats: 33.7g
- Protein: 15.2g

- Net Carb: 2.4g
- Fiber: 1.4g

# 13. SNACKS

**PREPARATION: 10 MIN**

**COOKING: 15 MIN**

**SERVES: 4**

# 131. CREAMY MANGO AND MINT DIP

## INGREDIENTS

- 1 Medium green chili, chopped
- 1 Medium white onion, peeled and chopped
- 1 tablespoon Grated ginger
- 1 teaspoon Minced garlic
- 1/8 teaspoon Salt
- 1/8 teaspoon Ground black pepper
- 1 teaspoon Cumin powder
- 1 teaspoon Mango powder
- 2 cups Mint leaves
- 1 cup Coriander leaves
- 4 tablespoons Cashew yogurt

## DIRECTIONS

1. Place all the ingredients for the dip in a blender and pulse for 1 to 2 minutes or until smooth.
2. Tip the dip into small cups and serve straightaway.

## NUTRITION

- Calories: 100
- Fat: 2g
- Fiber: 3g
- Carbs: 7g
- Protein: 5g

# 132. HOT RED CHILI AND GARLIC CHUTNEY

## INGREDIENTS

- 14 Red chilies, dried
- 5 teaspoons Minced garlic
- 1/8 teaspoon Salt
- 1 and ¼ cups Water

## DIRECTIONS

1. Place chilies in a bowl, pour in water and let rest for 20 minutes.
2. Then drain red chilies, chop them and add to a blender.
3. Add remaining ingredients into the blender and pulse for 1 to 2 minutes until smooth.
4. Tip the sauce into a bowl and serve straight away.

## NUTRITION

- Calories: 100
- Fat: 1g
- Fiber: 2g
- Carbs: 6g
- Protein: 7g

# 133. RED CHILIES AND ONION CHUTNEY

## INGREDIENTS

- 1 Medium white onion, peeled and chopped
- 1 teaspoon Minced garlic
- 2 Red chilies, chopped
- ¼ teaspoon Salt
- 1 teaspoon Sweet paprika
- 2 teaspoons Avocado oil
- ¼ cup Water

## DIRECTIONS

1. Place a medium skillet pan over medium-high heat, add oil and when hot, add onion, garlic, and chilies.
2. Cook onions for 5 minutes or until softened, then season with salt and paprika and pour in water.
3. Stir well and cook for 5 minutes.
4. Then spoon the chutney into a bowl and serve.

## NUTRITION

- Calories: 121
- Fat: 2g
- Fiber: 6g

- Carbs: 9g
- Protein: 5g

# 134. FAST GUACAMOLE

## INGREDIENTS

- 3 Medium avocados, peeled, pitted and cubed
- 1 Medium tomato, cubed
- ¼ cup Chopped cilantro
- 1 Medium red onion, peeled and chopped
- ½ teaspoon Salt
- ¼ teaspoon Ground white pepper
- 3 tablespoons Lime juice

## DIRECTIONS

1. Place all the ingredients for the salad in a medium bowl and stir until combined.
2. Serve guacamole straightaway as an appetizer.

## NUTRITION

- Calories: 87
- Fat: 4g
- Fiber: 4g
- Carbs: 8g
- Protein: 2g

**PREPARATION: 10 MIN**

**COOKING: 15 MIN**

**SERVES: 10**

# 135. COCONUT DILL DIP

## INGREDIENTS

- 1 tablespoon Chopped white onion
- 2 teaspoons Parsley flakes
- 2 teaspoons Chopped dill
- ¼ teaspoon Salt
- 1 cup Coconut cream
- ½ cup Avocado mayonnaise

## DIRECTIONS

1. Place all the ingredients for the dip in a medium bowl and whisk until combined.
2. Serve the dip with vegetable sticks as a side dish.

## NUTRITION

- Calories: 102
- Fat: 3g
- Fiber: 1g
- Carbs: 2g
- Protein: 2g

**PREPARATION: 5 MIN**

**COOKING: 10 MIN**

**SERVES: 12**

# 136. CREAMY CRAB DIP

## INGREDIENTS

- 1 pound Crab meat, chopped
- 2 tablespoons Chopped white onion
- 1 tablespoon Minced garlic
- 2 tablespoons Lemon juice
- 16 ounces Cream cheese, cubed
- 1/3 cup Avocado mayonnaise
- 2 tablespoons Grape juice

## DIRECTIONS

1. Place all the ingredients for the dip in a medium bowl and stir until combined.
2. Divide dip evenly between small bowls and serve as a party dip.

## NUTRITION

- Calories: 100
- Fat: 4g
- Fiber: 1g
- Carbs: 4g
- Protein: 4g

# 137. CREAMY CHEDDAR AND BACON SPREAD WITH ALMONDS

## INGREDIENTS

- 12 ounces Bacon, cooked and chopped
- 2 tablespoons Chopped sweet red pepper
- 1 Medium white onion, peeled and chopped
- ¾ teaspoon Salt
- ½ teaspoon Ground black pepper
- ½ cup Almonds, chopped
- 1 pound Cheddar cheese, grated
- 2 cups Avocado mayonnaise

## DIRECTIONS

1. Place all the ingredients for the dip in a medium bowl and stir until combined.
2. Divide dip evenly between small bowls and serve as a party dip.

## NUTRITION

- Calories: 184
- Fat: 12g
- Fiber: 1g
- Carbs: 4g
- Protein: 5g

# 138. GREEN TABASCO DEVILLED EGGS

## INGREDIENTS

- 6 Eggs
- 1/3 cup Mayonnaise
- 1 ½ tbsp. Green Tabasco
- Salt and Pepper, to taste

## DIRECTIONS

1. Place the eggs in a saucepan over medium heat and pour boiling water over, enough to cover them.
2. Cook for 6-8 minutes.
3. Place in an ice bath to cool.
4. When safe to handle, peel the eggs and slice them in half.
5. Scoop out the yolks and place in a bowl.
6. Add the remaining ingredients.
7. Whisk to combine.
8. Fill the egg holes with the mixture.
9. Serve and enjoy!

## NUTRITION

- Calories: 175
- Total Fats: 17g
- Net Carbs: 5g
- Protein: 6g
- Fiber: 1g

**PREPARATION: 30 MIN**

**COOKING: 10 MIN**

**SERVES: 20**

# 139. HERBED CHEESE BALLS

## INGREDIENTS

- 1/3 cup grated Parmesan Cheese
- 3 tbsp. Heavy Cream
- 4 tbsp. Butter, melted
- ¼ tsp Pepper
- 2 Eggs
- 1 cup Almond Flour
- ¼ cup Basil Leaves
- ¼ cup Parsley Leaves
- 2 tbsp. chopped Cilantro Leaves
- 1/3 cup crumbled Feta Cheese

## DIRECTIONS

1. Place the ingredients in your food processor.
2. Pulse until the mixture becomes smooth.
3. Transfer to a bowl and freeze for 20 minutes or so, to set.
4. Share the mixture into 20 balls.
5. Meanwhile, preheat the oven to 350 degrees F.
6. Arrange the cheese balls on a lined baking sheet.
7. Place in the oven and bake for 10 minutes.
8. Serve and enjoy!

## NUTRITION

- Calories: 60
- Total Fats: 5g
- Net Carbs: 8g
- Protein: 2g
- Fiber: 1g

**PREPARATION: 30 MIN**

**COOKING: 10 MIN**

**SERVES: 6**

# 140. CHEESY SALAMI SNACK

## INGREDIENTS

- 4 ounces Cream Cheese
- 7 ounces dried Salami
- ¼ cup chopped Parsley

## DIRECTIONS

1. Preheat the oven to 325 degrees F.
2. Slice the salami thinly (I got 30 slices).
3. Arrange the salami on a lined sheet and bake for 15 minutes.
4. Arrange on a serving platter and top each salami slice with a bit of cream cheese.
5. Serve and enjoy!

## NUTRITION

- Calories: 139
- Total Fats: 15g
- Net Carbs: 1g
- Protein: 9g
- Fiber: 0g

# 141. PESTO & OLIVE FAT BOMBS

## INGREDIENTS

- 1 cup Cream Cheese
- 10 Olives, sliced
- 2 tbsp. Pesto Sauce
- ½ cup grated Parmesan Cheese

## DIRECTIONS

1. Place all of the ingredients in a bowl.
2. Stir well to combine.
3. Place in the freezer and freeze for 15-20 minutes, to set.
4. Shape into 8 balls.
5. Serve and enjoy!

## NUTRITION

- Calories: 123
- Total Fats: 13g
- Net Carbs: 3g

- Protein: 4g
- Fiber: 3g

**PREPARATION: 25 MIN**

**COOKING: 10 MIN**

**SERVES: 4**

# 142. CHEESY BROCCOLI NUGGETS

## INGREDIENTS

- 1 cup shredded Cheese
- ¼ cup Almond Flour
- 2 cups Broccoli Florets, steamed in the microwave for 5 minutes
- 2 Egg Whites
- Salt and Pepper, to taste

## DIRECTIONS

1. Preheat the oven to 350 degrees F.
2. Place the broccoli florets in a bowl and mash them with a potato masher.
3. Add the remaining ingredients and mix well with your hands, until combined.
4. Line a baking sheet with parchment paper.
5. Drop 20 scoops of the mixture onto the sheet.
6. Place in the oven and bake for 20 minutes or until golden.
7. Serve and enjoy!

## NUTRITION

- Calories: 145
- Total Fats: 9g
- Net Carbs: 4g

- Protein: 10g
- Fiber: 1g

**PREPARATION: 90 MIN**

**COOKING: 50 MIN**

**SERVES: 6**

# 143. SALMON FAT BOMBS

## INGREDIENTS

- ½ cup Cream Cheese
- 1 ½ tbsp. chopped Dill
- 1 ¾ ounces Smoked Salmon, sliced
- 1 tbsp. Lemon Juice
- 1/3 cup Butter
- ¼ tsp Red Pepper Flakes
- ¼ tsp Garlic Powder
- Pinch of Salt
- ¼ tsp Pepper

## DIRECTIONS

1. Place the butter, salmon, lemon juice, and cream cheese, in your food processor.
2. Add the seasonings.
3. Pulse until smooth.
4. Drop spoonfuls of the mixture onto a lined dish.
5. Sprinkle with the dill.
6. Place in the fridge for about 80 minutes.
7. Serve and enjoy!

## NUTRITION

- Calories: 145
- Total Fats: 16g
- Net Carbs: 7g

- Protein: 3g
- Fiber: 1g

# 144. GUACAMOLE BACON BOMBS

## INGREDIENTS

- 1 tsp minced Garlic
- ¼ cup Butter
- ½ Avocado, flesh scooped out
- 1 tbsp. Lime Juice
- 1 tbsp. chopped Cilantro
- 4 Bacon Slices, cooked and crumbled
- 3 tbsp. diced Shallots
- Salt and Pepper, to taste
- 1 tbsp. minced Jalapeno

## DIRECTIONS

1. Place all of the ingredients, except the bacon, in your food processor.
2. Pulse until smooth. Alternatively, you can do this by whisking in a bowl. Just keep in mind that this way you will have chunks of garlic and jalapenos.
3. Transfer to a bowl and place in the freezer.
4. Freeze for 20 minutes, or until set.
5. Shape into 6 balls.
6. Coat them with bacon pieces.
7. Serve and enjoy!

## NUTRITION

- Calories: 155
- Total Fats: 15g
- Net Carbs: 4g
- Protein: 4g
- Fiber: 3g

# 14. POULTRY AND EGGS

**PREPARATION: 50 MIN**

**COOKING: 40 MIN**

**SERVES: 4**

# 145. CHEESE & SPINACH STUFFED CHICKEN

## INGREDIENTS

- 4 chicken breasts, boneless and skinless
- ½ cup mozzarella cheese
- 1 ½ cups Parmesan cheese, shredded
- 6 ounces cream cheese
- 2 cups spinach, chopped
- A pinch of nutmeg
- ½ tsp garlic, minced

**Breading:**
- 2 eggs, beaten
- 1/3 cup almond flour
- 2 tbsp. olive oil
- ½ tsp parsley
- 1/3 cup Parmesan cheese
- A pinch of onion powder

## DIRECTIONS

1. Pound the chicken until it doubles in size. Mix cream cheese, spinach, mozzarella cheese, nutmeg, and salt, pepper, and Parmesan cheese in a bowl. Divide the mixture between the chicken breasts and spread it out evenly. Wrap the chicken in a plastic wrap. Refrigerate for 15 minutes.
2. Preheat the oven to 370°F.
3. Beat the eggs and set aside. Combine all of the other breading ingredients in a bowl. Dip the chicken in eggs first, then in the breading mixture.
4. Warm the olive oil in a pan over medium heat. Cook the chicken in the pan until browned, about 5-6 minutes. Place on a lined baking sheet, and bake for 20 minutes. Serve.

## NUTRITION

- Calories: 491
- Net Carbs: 3.5g
- Fat: 36g

- Protein: 38g

**PREPARATION: 1H 30**

**COOKING: 40 MIN**

**SERVES: 6**

# 146. ASIAN CHICKEN WITH FRESH LIME-PEANUT SAUCE

## INGREDIENTS

- 1 tbsp. wheat-free soy sauce
- 1 tbsp. sugar-free fish sauce
- 1 tbsp. lime juice
- 1 tsp coriander
- 1 tsp garlic, minced
- 1 tsp ginger, minced
- 1 tbsp. olive oil
- 1 tbsp. rice wine vinegar
- 1 tsp cayenne pepper
- 1 tbsp. erythritol
- 6 chicken thighs

**Sauce:**
- ½ cup peanut butter
- 1 tsp garlic, minced
- 1 tbsp. lime juice
- 2 tbsp. water
- 1 tsp ginger, minced
- 1 tbsp. jalapeño, chopped
- 2 tbsp. rice wine vinegar
- 2 tbsp. erythritol
- 1 tbsp. fish sauce

## DIRECTIONS

1. Combine all of the chicken ingredients in a large Ziploc bag.
2. Seal the bag and shake to combine.
3. Refrigerate for about 1 hour.
4. Remove from the fridge about 15 minutes before cooking.
5. Preheat the grill to medium, and grill the chicken for about 7 minutes per side.
6. Meanwhile, whisk together all of the sauce ingredients in a mixing bowl.
7. Serve the chicken drizzled with peanut sauce.

## NUTRITION

- Calories: 492
- Net Carbs: 3g
- Fat: 36g

- Protein: 35g

**PREPARATION: 50 MIN**

**COOKING: 40 MIN**

**SERVES: 4**

# 147. BACON-WRAPPED CHICKEN WITH GRILLED ASPARAGUS

## INGREDIENTS

- 2 tbsp. fresh lemon juice
- 6 chicken breasts
- 8 bacon slices
- 1 tbsp. olive oil
- 1 lb. asparagus spears
- 3 tbsp. olive oil
- Salt and black pepper to taste
- Manchego cheese for topping

## DIRECTIONS

1. Preheat the oven to 400°F.
2. Season chicken breasts with salt and black pepper, and wrap 2 bacon slices around each chicken breast. Arrange on a baking sheet that is lined with parchment paper, drizzle with oil, and bake for 25-30 minutes until bacon is brown and crispy.
3. Preheat the grill.
4. Brush the asparagus spears with olive oil and season with salt. Grill turning frequently until slightly charred, 5-10 minutes.
5. Remove to a plate and drizzle with lemon juice. Grate over Manchego cheese so that it melts a little on contact with the hot asparagus and forms a cheesy dressing.

## NUTRITION

- Calories: 468
- Net Carbs: 2g
- Fat: 38g
- Protein: 26g

**PREPARATION: 15 MIN**

**COOKING: 40 MIN**

**SERVES: 4**

# 148. SPICY CHEESE CHICKEN SOUP

## INGREDIENTS

- ½ cup salsa enchilada verde
- 2 cups chicken, cooked and shredded
- 2 cups chicken or bone broth
- 1 cup cheddar cheese, shredded
- 4 ounces cream cheese
- ½ tsp chili powder
- ½ tsp cumin, ground
- ½ tsp fresh cilantro, chopped
- Salt and black pepper to taste

## DIRECTIONS

1. Combine the cream cheese, salsa verde, and broth in a food processor.
2. Pulse until smooth. Transfer the mixture to a pot and place over medium heat.
3. Cook until hot, but do not bring to a boil.
4. Add chicken, chili powder, and cumin, and cook for about 3-5 minutes, or until it is heated through. Stir in Cheddar cheese. Season with salt and pepper to taste.
5. Serve hot in individual bowls sprinkled with fresh cilantro.

## NUTRITION

- Calories: 346
- Net Carbs: 3g
- Fat: 23g

- Protein: 25g

# 149. BOK CHOY CAESAR SALAD WITH CHICKEN

## INGREDIENTS

- Chicken:
- 4 chicken thighs, boneless and skinless
- ¼ cup lemon juice
- 2 garlic cloves, minced
- 2 tbsp. olive oil

**Salad:**
- ½ cup caesar salad dressing, sugar-free
- 2 tbsp. olive oil
- 12 bok choy leaves
- 3 Parmesan cheese crisps
- Parmesan cheese, grated or garnishing

## DIRECTIONS

1. Combine the chicken ingredients in a Ziploc bag. Seal the bag, shake to combine, and refrigerate for 1 hour.
2. Preheat the grill to medium heat, and grill the chicken about 4 minutes per side.
3. Cut bok choy leaves lengthwise, and brush it with oil. Grill for about 3 minutes. Place on a serving platter. Top with the chicken, and drizzle the dressing over. Sprinkle with Parmesan cheese and finish with Parmesan crisps to serve.

## NUTRITION

- Calories: 529
- Net Carbs: 5g
- Fat: 39g
- Protein: 33g

# 150. CHICKEN & SPINACH GRATIN

## INGREDIENTS

- 6 chicken breasts, skinless and boneless
- 1 tsp mixed spice seasoning
- Pink salt and black pepper to season
- 2 loose cups baby spinach
- 3 tsp olive oil
- 4 oz. cream cheese, cubed
- 1 ¼ cups mozzarella cheese, shredded
- 4 tbsp. water

## DIRECTIONS

1. Preheat oven to 375°F.
2. Season chicken with spice mix, salt, and black pepper. Pat with your hands to have the seasoning stick on the chicken.
3. Put in the casserole dish and layer spinach over the chicken.
4. Mix the oil with cream cheese, mozzarella, salt, and black pepper and stir in water a tablespoon at a time.
5. Pour the mixture over the chicken and cover the pot with aluminum foil.
6. Bake for 20 minutes, remove foil and continue cooking for 15 minutes until a beautiful golden brown color is formed on top.
7. Take out and allow sitting for 5 minutes. Serve warm with braised asparagus.

## NUTRITION

- Calories: 340
- Net Carbs: 1g
- Fat: 30.2g

- Protein: 15g

**PREPARATION: 20 MINUTES+ 2 HOURS REFRIGERATION**

**COOKING: 10 MIN**

**SERVES: 6**

# 151. CHILI CHICKEN KABOBS WITH TAHINI DRESSING

## INGREDIENTS

- 3 tbsp. soy sauce
- 1 tbsp. ginger-garlic paste
- 2 tbsp. swerve brown sugar
- 2 tbsp. olive oil
- 3 chicken breasts, cut into bite-sized cubes
- ½ cup tahini
- ½ tsp garlic powder
- Salt and chili pepper to taste

## DIRECTIONS

1. In a bowl, whisk soy sauce, ginger-garlic paste, swerve brown sugar, chili pepper, and olive oil. Put the chicken in a zipper bag, pour the marinade over, seal, and shake for an even coat. Marinate in the fridge for 2 hours.
2. Preheat a grill to 400°F and thread the chicken on skewers. Cook for 10 minutes in total with three to four turnings to be golden brown. Plate them.
3. Mix the tahini, garlic powder, salt, and ¼ cup of warm water in a bowl. Serve the chicken skewers and tahini dressing with cauliflower fried rice.

## NUTRITION

- Calories: 225
- Net Carbs: 2g
- Fat: 17.4g
- Protein: 15g

# 152. CHICKEN WITH EGGPLANT & TOMATOES

## INGREDIENTS

- 2 tbsp. ghee
- 1 lb. chicken thighs
- Salt and black pepper to taste
- 2 garlic cloves, minced
- 1 (14 oz.) can whole tomatoes
- 1 eggplant, diced
- 10 fresh basil leaves, chopped + extra to garnish

## DIRECTIONS

1. Melt ghee in a saucepan over medium heat, season the chicken with salt and black pepper, and fry for 4 minutes on each side until golden brown. Remove the chicken onto a plate.
2. Sauté the garlic in the ghee for 2 minutes, pour in the tomatoes, and cook covered for 8 minutes. Include the eggplant and basil. Cook for 4 minutes.
3. Season the sauce with salt and black pepper, stir and add the chicken. Coat with sauce and simmer for 3 minutes.
4. Serve chicken with sauce on a bed of squash pasta garnished with basil.

## NUTRITION

- Calories: 468
- Net Carbs: 2g
- Fat: 39.5g

- Protein: 26g

# 153. TASTY CHICKEN WITH BRUSSEL SPROUTS

## INGREDIENTS

- 5 pounds whole chicken
- 1 bunch oregano
- 1 bunch thyme
- 1 tbsp. marjoram
- 1 tbsp. parsley
- 1 tbsp. olive oil
- 2 pounds Brussel sprouts
- 1 lemon
- 4 tbsp. butter

## DIRECTIONS

1. Preheat your oven to 450°F.
2. Stuff the chicken with oregano, thyme, and lemon.
3. Make sure the wings are tucked over and behind.
4. Roast for 15 minutes. Reduce the heat to 325°F, and cook for 40 minutes.
5. Spread the butter over the chicken and sprinkle parsley and marjoram.
6. Add the Brussel sprouts. Return to oven and bake for 40 more minutes.
7. Let sit for 10 minutes before carving.

## NUTRITION

- Calories: 430
- Net Carbs: 5g
- Fat: 32g

- Protein: 30g

**PREPARATION: 30 MIN**

**COOKING: 40 MIN**

**SERVES: 4**

# 154. WEEKEND CHICKEN WITH GRAPEFRUIT & LEMON

## INGREDIENTS

- 1 cup omission IPA
- A pinch of garlic powder
- 1 tsp grapefruit zest
- 3 tbsp. lemon juice
- ½ tsp coriander, ground
- 1 tbsp. fish sauce
- 2 tbsp. butter
- ¼ tsp xanthan gum
- 3 tbsp. swerve sweetener
- 20 chicken wing pieces
- Salt and black pepper to taste

## DIRECTIONS

1. Combine lemon juice and zest, fish sauce, coriander, omission IPA, sweetener, and garlic powder in a saucepan.
2. Bring to a boil, cover, lower the heat, and let simmer for 10 minutes.
3. Stir in the butter and xanthan gum. Set aside. Season the wings with some salt and pepper.
4. Preheat the grill and cook for 5 minutes per side.
5. Serve topped with the sauce.

## NUTRITION

- Calories: 365
- Net Carbs: 4g
- Fat: 25g

- Protein: 21g

**PREPARATION: 22 MIN**

**COOKING: 30 MIN**

**SERVES: 4**

# 155. ROSEMARY CHICKEN WITH AVOCADO SAUCE

## INGREDIENTS

- 1 avocado, pitted
- ½ cup mayonnaise
- 3 tbsp. ghee
- 4 chicken breasts
- Salt and black pepper to taste
- 1 cup rosemary, chopped
- ½ cup chicken broth

## DIRECTIONS

1. Spoon avocado, mayonnaise, and salt into a food processor and puree until a smooth sauce is derived. Adjust the taste with salt. Pour sauce into a jar and refrigerate.
2. Melt ghee in a large skillet, season chicken with salt and black pepper, and fry for 4 minutes on each side to a golden brown. Remove chicken to a plate.
3. Pour the broth in the same skillet and add the cilantro. Bring to simmer covered for 3 minutes and add the chicken. Cover, and cook on low heat for 5 minutes until the liquid has reduced and chicken is fragrant.
4. Dish chicken only into serving plates and spoon the mayo-avocado sauce over.
5. Serve warm with buttered green beans and baby carrots.

## NUTRITION

- Calories: 398
- Net Carbs: 4g
- Fat: 32g
- Protein: 24g

**PREPARATION: 30 MIN**

**COOKING: 40 MIN**

**SERVES: 4**

# 156. TURKEY PATTIES WITH CUCUMBER SALSA

## INGREDIENTS

- 2 spring onions, thinly sliced
- 1 pound turkey, ground
- 1 egg
- 2 garlic cloves, minced
- 1 tbsp. herbs, chopped
- 1 small chili pepper, deseeded and diced
- 2 tbsp. ghee
- Cucumber Salsa:
- 1 tbsp. apple cider vinegar
- 1 tbsp. dill, chopped
- 1 garlic clove, minced
- 2 cucumbers, grated
- 1 cup sour cream
- 1 jalapeño pepper, minced
- 2 tbsp. olive oil

## DIRECTIONS

1. Place all of the turkey ingredients, except the ghee, in a bowl. Mix to combine. Make patties out of the mixture.
2. Melt ghee in a skillet over medium heat. Cook the patties for 3 minutes per side.
3. Place all of the salsa ingredients in a bowl and mix to combine. Serve the patties topped with salsa.

## NUTRITION

- Calories: 475
- Net Carbs: 5g
- Fat: 38g

- Protein: 26g

**PREPARATION: 5 MIN**

**COOKING: 6 MIN**

**SERVES: 2**

# 157. PANCAKES

## INGREDIENTS

- ¼ cup almond flour
- 1 ½ tbsp. unsalted butter
- 2 oz. cream cheese, softened
- 2 eggs

## DIRECTIONS

1. Take a bowl, crack eggs in it, whisk well until fluffy, and then whisk in flour and cream cheese until well combined.
2. Take a skillet pan, place it over medium heat, add butter and when it melts, drop pancake batter in four sections, spread it evenly, and cook for 2 minutes per side until brown.
3. Serve.

## NUTRITION

- Calories: 166.8
- Fats: 15g
- Protein: 5.8g

- Net Carb: 1.8g
- Fiber: 0.8g

**PREPARATION: 5 MIN**

**COOKING: 0 MIN**

**SERVES: 2**

# 158. CHEESE ROLL-UPS

## INGREDIENTS

- 2 oz. mozzarella cheese, sliced, full-fat
- 1-ounce butter, unsalted

## DIRECTIONS

1. Cut cheese into slices and then cut butter into thin slices.
2. Top each cheese slice with a slice of butter, roll it and then serve.

## NUTRITION

- Calories: 166
- Fats: 15g
- Protein: 6.5g

- Net Carb: 2g
- Fiber: 0g

**PREPARATION: 5 MIN**

**COOKING: 5 MIN**

**SERVES: 2**

# 159. SCRAMBLED EGGS WITH SPINACH AND CHEESE

## INGREDIENTS

- 2 oz. spinach
- 2 eggs
- 1 tbsp. coconut oil
- 2 tbsp. grated mozzarella cheese, full-fat

**Seasoning:**
- ¼ tsp salt
- 1/8 tsp ground black pepper
- 1/8 tsp red pepper flakes

## DIRECTIONS

1. Take a medium bowl, crack eggs in it, add salt and black pepper and whisk until combined.
2. Take a medium skillet pan, place it over medium heat, add oil and when hot, add spinach and cook for 1 minute until leaves wilt.
3. Pour eggs over spinach, stir and cook for 1 minute until just set.
4. Stir in cheese, then remove the pan from heat and sprinkle red pepper flakes on top.
5. Serve.

## NUTRITION

- Calories: 171
- Fats: 14g
- Protein: 9.2g
- Net Carb: 1.1g
- Fiber: 1.7g

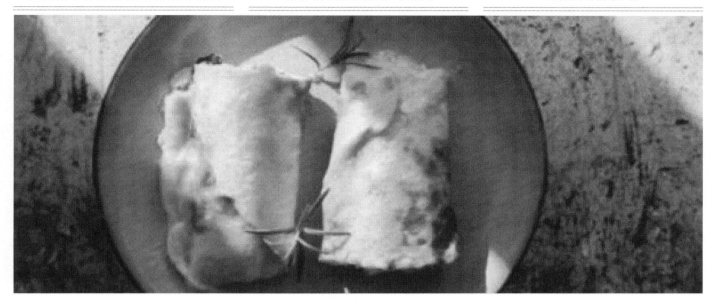

# 160. EGG WRAPS

## INGREDIENTS

- 2 eggs
- 1 tbsp. coconut oil

**Seasoning:**
- ¼ tsp salt
- 1/8 tsp ground black pepper

## DIRECTIONS

1. Take a medium bowl, crack eggs in it, add salt and black pepper, and then whisk until blended.
2. Take a frying pan, place it over medium-low heat, add coconut oil and when it melts, pour in half of the egg, spread it evenly into a thin layer by rotating the pan and cook for 2 minutes.
3. Then flip the pan, cook for 1 minute, and transfer to a plate.
4. Repeat with the remaining egg to make another wrap, then roll each egg wrap and serve.

## NUTRITION

- Calories: 68
- Fats: 4.7g
- Protein: 5.5g

- Net Carb: 0.5g
- Fiber: 0g

# 161. CHAFFLES WITH POACHED EGGS

## INGREDIENTS

- 2 tsp coconut flour
- ½ cup shredded cheddar cheese, full-fat
- 3 eggs

**Seasoning:**
- ¼ tsp salt
- 1/8 tsp ground black pepper

## DIRECTIONS

1. Switch on a mini waffle maker and let it preheat for 5 minutes.
2. Meanwhile, take a medium bowl, place all the ingredients in it, reserving 2 eggs and then mix by using an immersion blender until smooth.
3. Ladle the batter evenly into the waffle maker, shut with lid, and let it cook for 3 to 4 minutes until firm and golden brown.
4. Meanwhile, prepare poached eggs, and for this, take a medium bowl half full with water, place it over medium heat and bring it to a boil.
5. Then crack an egg in a ramekin, carefully pour it into the boiling water and cook for 3 minutes.
6. Transfer egg to a plate lined with paper towels by using a slotted spoon and repeat with the other egg.
7. Top chaffles with poached eggs, season with salt and black pepper, and then serve.

## NUTRITION

- Calories: 265
- Fats: 18.5g
- Protein: 17.6g

- Net Carb: 3.4g
- Fiber: 6g

**PREPARATION: 5 MIN**

**COOKING: 10 MIN**

**SERVES: 2**

# 162. CHAFFLE WITH SCRAMBLED EGGS

## INGREDIENTS

- 2 tsp coconut flour
- ½ cup shredded cheddar cheese, full-fat
- 3 eggs
- 1-ounce butter, unsalted

**Seasoning:**
- ¼ tsp salt
- 1/8 tsp ground black pepper
- 1/8 tsp dried oregano

## DIRECTIONS

1. Switch on a mini waffle maker and let it preheat for 5 minutes.
2. Meanwhile, take a medium bowl, place all the ingredients in it, reserving 2 eggs and then mix by using an immersion blender until smooth.
3. Ladle the batter evenly into the waffle maker, shut with lid, and let it cook for 3 to 4 minutes until firm and golden brown.
4. Meanwhile, prepare scrambled eggs and for this, take a medium bowl, crack the eggs in it and whisk them with a fork until frothy, and then season with salt and black pepper.
5. Take a medium skillet pan, place it over medium heat, add butter and when it melts, pour in eggs and cook for 2 minutes until creamy, stirring continuously.
6. Top chaffles with scrambled eggs, sprinkle with oregano, and then serve.

### NUTRITION

- Calories: 265
- Fats: 18.5g
- Protein: 17.6g

- Net Carb: 3.4g
- Fiber: 6g

**PREPARATION: 5 MIN**

 **COOKING: 12 MIN**

 **SERVES: 2**

# 163. SHEET PAN EGGS WITH MUSHROOMS AND SPINACH

## INGREDIENTS

- 2 eggs
- 1 tsp chopped jalapeno pepper
- 1 tbsp. chopped mushrooms
- 1 tbsp. chopped spinach
- 1 tbsp. chopped chard

**Seasoning:**
- 1/3 tsp salt
- 1/4 tsp ground black pepper

## DIRECTIONS

1. Turn on the oven, then set it to 350 degrees F and let it preheat.
2. Take a medium bowl, crack eggs in it, add salt and black pepper, then add all the vegetables and stir until combined.
3. Take a medium sheet ball or rimmed baking sheet, grease it with oil, pour prepared egg batter on it, and then bake for 10 to 12 minutes until done.
4. Cut egg into two squares and then serve.

## NUTRITION

- Calories: 165
- Fats: 10.7g
- Protein: 14g
- Net Carb: 1.5g
- Fiber: 0.5g

**PREPARATION: 10 MIN**

**COOKING: 15 MIN**

**SERVES: 2**

# 164. NO BREAD BREAKFAST SANDWICH

## INGREDIENTS

- 2 slices of ham
- 4 eggs
- 1 tsp tabasco sauce
- 3 tbsp. butter, unsalted
- 2 tsp grated mozzarella cheese

**Seasoning:**
- ¼ tsp salt
- 1/8 tsp ground black pepper

## DIRECTIONS

1. Take a frying pan, place it over medium heat, add butter and when it melt, crack an egg in it and fry for 2 to 3 minutes until cooked to desired level.
2. Transfer fried egg to a plate, fry remaining eggs in the same manner and when done, season eggs with salt and black pepper.
3. Prepare the sandwich and for this, use a fried egg as a base for sandwich, then top with a ham slice, sprinkle with a tsp of ham and cover with another fried egg.
4. Place egg into the pan, return it over low heat and let it cook until cheese melts.
5. Prepare another sandwich in the same manner and then serve.

## NUTRITION

- Calories: 180
- Fats: 15g
- Protein: 10g

- Net Carb: 1g
- Fiber: 0g

# 165. SCRAMBLED EGGS WITH BASIL AND BUTTER

## INGREDIENTS

- 1 tbsp. chopped basil leaves
- 2 tbsp. butter, unsalted
- 2 tbsp. grated cheddar cheese
- 2 eggs
- 2 tbsp. whipping cream

**Seasoning:**
- 1/8 tsp salt
- 1/8 tsp ground black pepper

## DIRECTIONS

1. Take a medium bowl, crack eggs in it, add salt, black pepper, cheese and cream and whisk until combined.
2. Take a medium pan, place it over low heat, add butter and when it melts, pour in the egg mixture and cook for 2 to 3 minutes until eggs have scrambled to the desired level.
3. When done, distribute scrambled eggs between two plates, top with basil leaves and then serve.

## NUTRITION

- Calories: 320
- Fats: 29g
- Protein: 13g
- Net Carb: 1.5g
- Fiber: 0g

# 166. BACON, AND EGGS

## INGREDIENTS

- 2 eggs
- 4 slices of turkey bacon
- ¼ tsp salt
- ¼ tsp ground black pepper

## DIRECTIONS

1. Take a skillet pan, place it over medium heat, add bacon slices in it and cook for 5 minutes until crispy.
2. Transfer bacon slices to a plate and set aside until required, reserving the fat in the pan.
3. Cook the egg in the pan one at a time, and for this, crack an egg in the pan and cook for 2 to 3 minutes or more until the egg has cooked to desire level.
4. Transfer egg to a plate and cook the other egg in the same manner.
5. Season eggs with salt and black pepper and then serve with cooked bacon.

## NUTRITION

- Calories: 136
- Fats: 11g
- Protein: 7.5g

- Net Carb: 1g
- Fiber: 0g

**PREPARATION: 5 MIN**

**COOKING: 10 MIN**

**SERVES: 2**

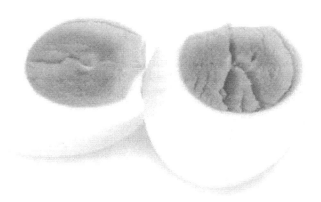

# 167. BOILED EGGS

## INGREDIENTS

- 2 eggs
- ½ of a medium avocado

**Seasoning:**
- ¼ tsp salt
- ¼ tsp ground black pepper

## DIRECTIONS

1. Place a medium pot over medium heat, fill it half full with water and bring it to boil.
2. Then carefully place the eggs in the boiling water and boil the eggs for 5 minutes until soft-boiled, 8 minutes for medium-boiled, and 10 minutes for hard-boiled.
3. When eggs have boiled, transfer them to a bowl containing chilled water and let them rest for 5 minutes.
4. Then crack the eggs with a spoon and peel them.
5. Cut each egg into slices, season with salt and black pepper, and serve with diced avocado.

## NUTRITION

- Calories: 112
- Fats: 9.5g
- Protein: 5.5g

- Net Carb: 1g
- Fiber: 0g

# 15. MEAT

# 168. BEEF WITH CABBAGE NOODLES

## INGREDIENTS

- 4 oz. ground beef
- 1 cup chopped cabbage
- 4 oz. tomato sauce
- ½ tsp minced garlic
- ½ cup of water

**Seasoning:**
- ½ tbsp. coconut oil
- ½ tsp salt
- ¼ tsp Italian seasoning
- 1/8 tsp dried basil

## DIRECTIONS

1. Take a skillet pan, place it over medium heat, add oil and when hot, add beef and cook for 5 minutes until nicely browned.
2. Meanwhile, prepare the cabbage and for it, slice the cabbage into thin shred.
3. When the beef has cooked, add garlic, season with salt, basil, and Italian seasoning, stir well and continue cooking for 3 minutes until beef has thoroughly cooked.
4. Pour in tomato sauce and water, stir well and bring the mixture to boil.
5. Then reduce heat to medium-low level, add cabbage, stir well until well mixed and simmer for 3 to 5 minutes until cabbage is softened, covering the pan.
6. Uncover the pan and continue simmering the beef until most of the cooking liquid has evaporated.
7. Serve.

## NUTRITION

- Calories: 188.5
- Fats: 12.5g
- Protein: 15.5g

- Net Carb: 2.5g
- Fiber: 1g

**PREPARATION: 5 MIN**

**COOKING: 0 MIN**

**SERVES: 2**

# 169. ROAST BEEF AND MOZZARELLA PLATE

## INGREDIENTS

- 4 slices of roast beef
- ½ ounce chopped lettuce
- 1 avocado, pitted
- 2 oz. mozzarella cheese, cubed
- ½ cup mayonnaise

**Seasoning:**
- ¼ tsp salt
- 1/8 tsp ground black pepper
- 2 tbsp. avocado oil

## DIRECTIONS

1. Scoop out flesh from avocado and divide it evenly between two plates.
2. Add slices of roast beef, lettuce, and cheese and then sprinkle with salt and black pepper.
3. Serve with avocado oil and mayonnaise.

## NUTRITION

- Calories: 267.7
- Fats: 24.5g
- Protein: 9.5g

- Net Carb: 1.5g
- Fiber: 2g

# 170. BEEF AND BROCCOLI

## INGREDIENTS

- 6 slices of beef roast, cut into strips
- 1 scallion, chopped
- 3 oz. broccoli florets, chopped
- 1 tbsp. avocado oil
- 1 tbsp. butter, unsalted

**Seasoning:**
- ¼ tsp salt
- 1/8 tsp ground black pepper
- 1 ½ tbsp. soy sauce
- 3 tbsp. chicken broth

## DIRECTIONS

1. Take a medium skillet pan, place it over medium heat, add oil and when hot, add beef strips and cook for 2 minutes until hot.
2. Transfer beef to a plate, add scallion to the pan, then add butter and cook for 3 minutes until tender.
3. Add remaining ingredients, stir until mixed, switch heat to the low level and simmer for 3 to 4 minutes until broccoli is tender.
4. Return beef to the pan, stir until well combined and cook for 1 minute.
5. Serve.

## NUTRITION

- Calories: 245
- Fats: 15.7g
- Protein: 21.6g

- Net Carb: 1.7g
- Fiber: 1.3g

**PREPARATION: 5 MIN**

**COOKING: 10 MIN**

**SERVES: 2**

# 171. GARLIC HERB BEEF ROAST

## INGREDIENTS

- 6 slices of beef roast
- ½ tsp garlic powder
- 1/3 tsp dried thyme
- ¼ tsp dried rosemary
- 2 tbsp. butter, unsalted

**Seasoning:**

- 1/3 tsp salt
- ¼ tsp ground black pepper

## DIRECTIONS

1. Prepare the spice mix and for this, take a small bowl, place garlic powder, thyme, rosemary, salt, and black pepper and then stir until mixed.
2. Sprinkle spice mix on the beef roast.
3. Take a medium skillet pan, place it over medium heat, add butter and when it melts, add beef roast and then cook for 5 to 8 minutes until golden brown and cooked.
4. Serve.

## NUTRITION

- Calories: 140
- Fats: 12.7g
- Protein: 5.5g

- Net Carb: 0.1g
- Fiber: 0.2g

# 172. SPROUTS STIR-FRY WITH KALE, BROCCOLI, AND BEEF

## INGREDIENTS

- 3 slices of beef roast, chopped
- 2 oz. Brussels sprouts, halved
- 4 oz. broccoli florets
- 3 oz. kale
- 1 ½ tbsp. butter, unsalted
- 1/8 tsp red pepper flakes

**Seasoning:**
- ¼ tsp garlic powder
- ¼ tsp salt
- 1/8 tsp ground black pepper

## DIRECTIONS

1. Take a medium skillet pan, place it over medium heat, add ¾ tbsp. butter and when it melts, add broccoli florets and sprouts, sprinkle with garlic powder, and cook for 2 minutes.
2. Season vegetables with salt and red pepper flakes, add chopped beef, stir until mixed and continue cooking for 3 minutes until browned on one side.
3. Then add kale along with remaining butter, flip the vegetables and cook for 2 minutes until kale leaves wilts.
4. Serve.

## NUTRITION

- Calories: 125
- Fats: 9.4g
- Protein: 4.8g

- Net Carb: 1.7g
- Fiber: 2.6g

# 173. BEEF AND VEGETABLE SKILLET

## INGREDIENTS

- 3 oz. spinach, chopped
- ½ pound ground beef
- 2 slices of bacon, diced
- 2 oz. chopped asparagus

**Seasoning:**

- 3 tbsp. coconut oil
- 2 tsp dried thyme
- 2/3 tsp salt
- ½ tsp ground black pepper

## DIRECTIONS

1. Take a skillet pan, place it over medium heat, add oil and when hot, add beef and bacon and cook for 5 to 7 minutes until slightly browned.
2. Then add asparagus and spinach, sprinkle with thyme, stir well and cook for 7 to 10 minutes until thoroughly cooked.
3. Season skillet with salt and black pepper and serve.

## NUTRITION

- Calories: 332.5
- Fats: 26g
- Protein: 23.5g

- Net Carb: 1.5g
- Fiber: 1g

# 174. BEEF, PEPPER AND GREEN BEANS STIR-FRY

## INGREDIENTS

- 6 oz. ground beef
- 2 oz. chopped green bell pepper
- 4 oz. green beans
- 3 tbsp. grated cheddar cheese

**Seasoning:**

- ½ tsp salt
- ¼ tsp ground black pepper
- ¼ tsp paprika

## DIRECTIONS

1. Take a skillet pan, place it over medium heat, add ground beef and cook for 4 minutes until slightly browned.
2. Then add bell pepper and green beans, season with salt, paprika, and black pepper, stir well and continue cooking for 7 to 10 minutes until beef and vegetables have cooked through.
3. Sprinkle cheddar cheese on top, then transfer pan under the broiler and cook for 2 minutes until cheese has melted and the top is golden brown.
4. Serve.

## NUTRITION

- Calories: 282.5
- Fats: 17.6g
- Protein: 26.1g

- Net Carb: 2.9g
- Fiber: 2.1g

# 175. CHEESY MEATLOAF

## INGREDIENTS

- 4 oz. ground turkey
- 1 egg
- 1 tbsp. grated mozzarella cheese
- ¼ tsp Italian seasoning
- ½ tbsp. soy sauce

**Seasoning:**
- ¼ tsp salt
- 1/8 tsp ground black pepper

## DIRECTIONS

1. Take a bowl, place all the ingredients in it, and stir until mixed.
2. Take a heatproof mug, spoon in prepared mixture and microwave for 3 minutes at high heat setting until cooked.
3. When done, let meatloaf rest in the mug for 1 minute, then take it out, cut it into two slices and serve.

## NUTRITION

- Calories: 196.5
- Fats: 13.5g
- Protein: 18.7g

- Net Carb: 18.7g
- Fiber: 0g

**PREPARATION: 10 MIN**

**COOKING: 10 MIN**

**SERVES: 2**

# 176. ROAST BEEF AND VEGETABLE PLATE

## INGREDIENTS

- 2 scallions, chopped in large pieces
- 1 ½ tbsp. coconut oil
- 4 thin slices of roast beef
- 4 oz. cauliflower and broccoli mix
- 1 tbsp. butter, unsalted

**Seasoning:**
- ½ tsp salt
- 1/3 tsp ground black pepper
- 1 tsp dried parsley

## DIRECTIONS

1. Turn on the oven, then set it to 400 degrees F, and let it preheat.
2. Take a baking sheet, grease it with oil, place slices of roast beef on one side, and top with butter.
3. Take a separate bowl, add cauliflower and broccoli mix, add scallions, drizzle with oil, season with remaining salt and black pepper, toss until coated and then spread vegetables on the empty side of the baking sheet.
4. Bake for 5 to 7 minutes until beef is nicely browned and vegetables are tender-crisp, tossing halfway.
5. Distribute beef and vegetables between two plates and then serve.

## NUTRITION

- Calories: 313
- Fats: 26g
- Protein: 15.6g

- Net Carb: 2.8g
- Fiber: 1.9g

# 177. STEAK AND CHEESE PLATE

## INGREDIENTS

- 1 green onion, chopped
- 2 oz. chopped lettuce
- 2 beef steaks
- 2 oz. of cheddar cheese, sliced
- ½ cup mayonnaise

**Seasoning:**
- ¼ tsp salt
- 1/8 tsp ground black pepper
- 3 tbsp. avocado oil

## DIRECTIONS

1. Prepare the steak, and for this, season it with salt and black pepper.
2. Take a medium skillet pan, place it over medium heat, add oil and when hot, add seasoned steaks, and cook for 7 to 10 minutes until cooked to the desired level.
3. When done, distribute steaks between two plates, add scallion, lettuce, and cheese slices.
4. Drizzle with remaining oil and then serve with mayonnaise.

## NUTRITION

- Calories: 714
- Fats: 65.3g
- Protein: 25.3g
- Net Carb: 4g
- Fiber: 5.3g

# 178. GARLICKY STEAKS WITH ROSEMARY

## INGREDIENTS

- 2 beef steaks
- ¼ of a lime, juiced
- 1 ½ tsp garlic powder
- ¾ tsp dried rosemary
- 2 ½ tbsp. avocado oil

**Seasoning:**
- ½ tsp salt
- ¼ tsp ground black pepper

## DIRECTIONS

1. Prepare steaks, and for this, sprinkle garlic powder on all sides of steak.
2. Take a shallow dish, place 1 ½ tbsp. oil and lime juice in it, whisk until combined, add steaks, turn to coat and let it marinate for 20 minutes at room temperature.
3. Then take a griddle pan, place it over medium-high heat and grease it with remaining oil.
4. Season marinated steaks with salt and black pepper, add to the griddle pan and cook for 7 to 12 minutes until cooked to the desired level.
5. When done, wrap steaks in foil for 5 minutes, then cut into slices across the grain.
6. Sprinkle rosemary over steaks slices and then serve.

## NUTRITION

- Calories: 213
- Fats: 13g
- Protein: 22g

- Net Carb: 1g
- Fiber: 0g

# 16. SEAFOOD

**PREPARATION: 5 MIN**

**COOKING: 10 MIN**

**SERVES: 2**

# 179. FISH AND EGG PLATE

## INGREDIENTS

- 2 eggs
- 1 tbsp. butter, unsalted
- 2 pacific whitening fillets
- ½ oz. chopped lettuce
- 1 scallion, chopped

**Seasoning:**
- 3 tbsp. avocado oil
- 1/3 tsp salt
- 1/3 tsp ground black pepper

## DIRECTIONS

1. Cook the eggs and for this, take a frying pan, place it over medium heat, add butter and when it melts, crack the egg in the pan and cook for 2 to 3 minutes until fried to desired liking.
2. Transfer fried egg to a plate and then cook the remaining egg in the same manner.
3. Meanwhile, season fish fillets with ¼ tsp each of salt and black pepper.
4. When eggs have fried, sprinkle salt and black pepper on them, then add 1 tbsp. oil into the frying pan, add fillets and cook for 4 minutes per side until thoroughly cooked.
5. When done, distribute fillets to the plate, add lettuce and scallion, drizzle with remaining oil, and then serve.

## NUTRITION

- Calories: 485
- Fat: 33g
- Fiber: 6g
- Carbs: 5g
- Protein: 39g

# 180. SESAME TUNA SALAD

## INGREDIENTS

- 6 oz. of tuna in water
- ½ tbsp. chili-garlic paste
- ½ tbsp. black sesame seeds, toasted
- 2 tbsp. mayonnaise
- 1 tbsp. sesame oil

**Seasoning:**
- 1/8 tsp red pepper flakes

## DIRECTIONS

1. Take a medium bowl, all the ingredients for the salad in it except for tuna, and then stir until well combined.
2. Fold in tuna until mixed and then refrigerator for 30 minutes.
3. Serve.

## NUTRITION

- Calories: 322
- Fats: 25.4g
- Protein: 17.7g

- Net Carb: 2.6g
- Fiber: 3g

**PREPARATION: 10 MIN**

**COOKING: 10 MIN**

**SERVES: 2**

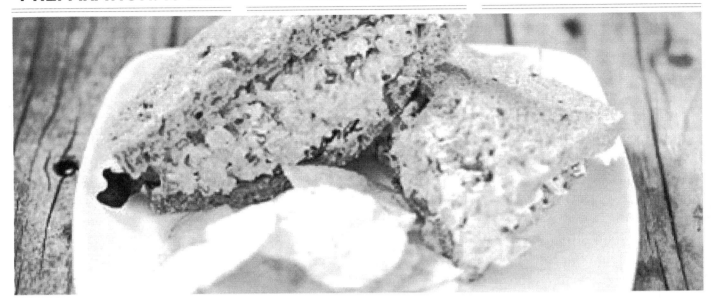

# 181. KETO TUNA SANDWICH

## INGREDIENTS

- 2 oz. tuna, packed in water
- 2 2/3 tbsp. coconut flour
- 1 tsp baking powder
- 2 eggs
- 2 tbsp. mayonnaise

**Seasoning:**
- ¼ tsp salt
- ¼ tsp ground black pepper

## DIRECTIONS

1. Turn on the oven, then set it to 375 degrees F and let it preheat.
2. Meanwhile, prepare the batter for this, add all the ingredients in a bowl, reserving mayonnaise, 1 egg, and 1/8 tsp salt, and then whisk until well combined.
3. Take a 4 by 4 inches heatproof baking pan, grease it with oil, pour in the prepared batter and bake 10 minutes until bread is firm.
4. Meanwhile, prepare tuna and for this, place tuna in a medium bowl, add mayonnaise, season with remaining salt and black pepper, and then stir until combined.
5. When done, let the bread cool in the pan for 5 minutes, then transfer it to a wire rack and cool for 20 minutes.
6. Slice the bread, prepare sandwiches with prepared tuna mixture, and then serve.

## NUTRITION

- Calories: 255
- Fats: 17.8g
- Protein: 16.3g
- Net Carb: 3.7g
- Fiber: 3.3g

**PREPARATION: 5 MIN**

**COOKING: 10 MIN**

**SERVES: 2**

# 182. TUNA MELT JALAPENO PEPPERS

## INGREDIENTS

- 4 jalapeno peppers
- 1-ounce tuna, packed in water
- 1-ounce cream cheese softened
- 1 tbsp. grated parmesan cheese
- 1 tbsp. grated mozzarella cheese

**Seasoning:**

- 1 tsp chopped dill pickles
- 1 green onion, green part sliced only

## DIRECTIONS

1. Turn on the oven, then set it to 400 degrees F and let it preheat.
2. Prepare the peppers and for this, cut each pepper in half lengthwise and remove seeds and stem.
3. Take a small bowl, place tuna in it, add remaining ingredients except for cheeses, and then stir until combined.
4. Spoon tuna mixture into peppers, sprinkle cheeses on top, and then bake for 7 to 10 minutes until cheese has turned golden brown.
5. Serve.

## NUTRITION

- Calories: 104
- Fats: 6.2g
- Protein: 7g

- Net Carb: 2.1g
- Fiber: 1.1g

# 183. SMOKED SALMON FAT BOMBS

## INGREDIENTS

- 2 tbsp. cream cheese, softened
- 1 ounce smoked salmon
- 2 tsp bagel seasoning

## DIRECTIONS

1. Take a medium bowl, place cream cheese and salmon in it, and stir until well combined.
2. Shape the mixture into bowls, roll them into bagel seasoning and then serve.

## NUTRITION

- Calories: 65
- Fats: 4.8g
- Protein: 4g

- Net Carb: 0.5g
- Fiber: 0g

# 184. SALMON CUCUMBER ROLLS

## INGREDIENTS

- 1 large cucumber
- 2 oz. smoked salmon
- 4 tbsp. mayonnaise
- 1 tsp sesame seeds

**Seasoning:**
- ¼ tsp salt
- ¼ tsp ground black pepper

## DIRECTIONS

1. Trim the ends of the cucumber, cut it into slices by using a vegetable peeler, and then place half of the cucumber slices in a dish.
2. Cover with paper towels, layer with remaining cucumber slices, top with paper towels, and let them refrigerate for 5 minutes.
3. Meanwhile, take a medium bowl, place salmon in it, add mayonnaise, season with salt and black pepper, and then stir until well combined.
4. Remove cucumber slices from the refrigerator, place salmon on one side of each cucumber slice, and then roll tightly.
5. Repeat with remaining cucumber, sprinkle with sesame seeds and then serve.

## NUTRITION

- Calories: 269
- Fats: 24g
- Protein: 6.7g

- Net Carb: 4g
- Fiber: 2g

**PREPARATION: 10 MIN**

**COOKING: 12 MIN**

**SERVES: 2**

# 185. BACON WRAPPED MAHI-MAHI

## INGREDIENTS

- 2 fillets of mahi-mahi
- 2 strips of bacon
- ½ of lime, zested
- 4 basil leaves
- ½ tsp salt

**Seasoning:**
- ½ tsp ground black pepper
- 1 tbsp. avocado oil

## DIRECTIONS

1. Turn on the oven, then set it to 375 degrees F and let them preheat.
2. Meanwhile, season fillets with salt and black pepper, top each fillet with 2 basil leaves, sprinkle with lime zest, wrap with a bacon strip and secure with a toothpick if needed.
3. Take a medium skillet pan, place it over medium-high heat, add oil and when hot, place prepared fillets in it and cook for 2 minutes per side.
4. Transfer pan into the oven and bake the fish for 5 to 7 minutes until thoroughly cooked.
5. Serve.

## NUTRITION

- Calories: 217
- Fats: 11.3g
- Protein: 27.1g
- Net Carb: 1.2g
- Fiber: 0.5g

# 186. CHEESY GARLIC BREAD WITH SMOKED SALMON

## INGREDIENTS

- 4 tbsp. almond flour
- ½ tsp baking powder
- 2 tbsp. grated cheddar cheese
- 1 egg
- 2 oz. salmon, cut into thin sliced

**Seasoning:**
- 1 tbsp. butter, unsalted
- ¼ tsp garlic powder
- 1/8 tsp salt
- ¼ tsp Italian seasoning

## DIRECTIONS

1. Take a heatproof bowl, place all the ingredients in it except for cheese and then stir by using a fork until well combined.
2. Fold in cheese until just mixed and then microwave for 1 minute at high heat setting until thoroughly cooked, else continue cooking for another 15 to 30 seconds.
3. When done, lift out the bread, cool it for 5 minutes and then cut it into slices.
4. Top each slice with salmon and then serve straight away

## NUTRITION

- Calories: 233
- Fats: 18g
- Protein: 13.8g

- Net Carb: 1.9g
- Fiber: 1.5g

# 187. SMOKED SALMON PASTA SALAD

## INGREDIENTS

- 1 zucchini, spiralized into noodles
- 4 oz. smoked salmon, break into pieces
- 2 oz. cream cheese
- 2 oz. mayonnaise
- 2 oz. sour cream

**Seasoning:**

- 1/3 tsp salt
- ¼ tsp ground black pepper
- ¼ tsp hot sauce

## DIRECTIONS

1. Take a medium bowl, place cream cheese in it, add mayonnaise, sour cream, salt, black pepper and hot sauce and stir until well combined.
2. Add zucchini noodles, toss until well coated and then fold in salmon until just mixed.
3. Serve.

## NUTRITION

- Calories: 458
- Fats: 38.7g
- Protein: 15.4g

- Net Carb: 6.1g
- Fiber: 1.7g

# 188. TUNA SALAD PICKLE BOATS

## INGREDIENTS

- 4 dill pickles
- 4 oz. of tuna, packed in water, drained
- ¼ of lime, juiced
- 4 tbsp. mayonnaise

**Seasoning:**

- ¼ tsp salt
- 1/8 tsp ground black pepper
- ¼ tsp paprika
- 1 tbsp. mustard paste

## DIRECTIONS

1. Prepare tuna salad and for this, take a medium bowl, place tuna in it, add lime juice, mayonnaise, salt, black pepper, paprika, and mustard and stir until mixed.
2. Cut each pickle into half lengthwise, scoop out seeds, and then fill with tuna salad.
3. Serve.

## NUTRITION

- Calories: 308.5
- Fats: 23.7g
- Protein: 17g

- Net Carb: 3.8g
- Fiber: 3.1g

**PREPARATION: 5 MIN**

**COOKING: 0 MIN**

**SERVES: 2**

# 189. SHRIMP DEVILED EGGS

## INGREDIENTS

- 2 eggs, boiled
- 2 oz. shrimps, cooked, chopped
- ½ tsp tabasco sauce
- ½ tsp mustard paste
- 2 tbsp. mayonnaise

**Seasoning:**
- 1/8 tsp salt
- 1/8 tsp ground black pepper

## DIRECTIONS

1. Peel the boiled eggs, then slice in half lengthwise and transfer egg yolks to a medium bowl by using a spoon.
2. Mash the egg yolk, add remaining ingredients and stir until well combined.
3. Spoon the egg yolk mixture into egg whites, and then serve.

## NUTRITION

- Calories: 210
- Fats: 16.4g
- Protein: 14g

- Net Carb: 1g
- Fiber: 0.1g

**PREPARATION: 5 MIN**

**COOKING: 10 MIN**

**SERVES: 2**

# 190. HERB CRUSTED TILAPIA

## INGREDIENTS

- 2 fillets of tilapia
- ½ tsp garlic powder
- ½ tsp Italian seasoning
- ½ tsp dried parsley
- 1/3 tsp salt

**Seasoning:**
- 2 tbsp. melted butter, unsalted
- 1 tbsp. avocado oil

## DIRECTIONS

1. Turn on the broiler and then let it preheat.
2. Meanwhile, take a small bowl, place melted butter in it, stir in oil and garlic powder until mixed, and then brush this mixture over tilapia fillets.
3. Stir together remaining spices and then sprinkle them generously on tilapia until well coated.
4. Place seasoned tilapia in a baking pan, place the pan under the broiler and then bake for 10 minutes until tender and golden, brushing with garlic-butter every 2 minutes.
5. Serve.

## NUTRITION

- Calories: 520
- Fats: 35g
- Protein: 36.2g

- Net Carb: 13.6g
- Fiber: 0.6g

# 191. TUNA STUFFED AVOCADO

## INGREDIENTS

- 1 medium avocado
- ¼ of a lemon, juiced
- 5-ounce tuna, packed in water
- 1 green onion, chopped
- 2 slices of turkey bacon, cooked, crumbled

**Seasoning:**
- ¼ tsp salt
- ¼ tsp ground black pepper

## DIRECTIONS

1. Drain tuna, place it in a bowl, and then broke it into pieces with a form.
2. Add remaining ingredients, except for avocado and bacon, and stir until well combined.
3. Cut avocado into half, remove its pit and then stuff its cavity evenly with the tuna mixture.
4. Top stuffed avocados with bacon and Serve.

## NUTRITION

- Calories: 108.5
- Fats: 8g
- Protein: 6g

- Net Carb: 0.8g
- Fiber: 2.3g

# 17. DESSERTS

# 192. WALNUT COOKIES

## INGREDIENTS

- ¼ cup coconut flour
- 8 tablespoon butter
- ½ cup erythritol
- 1 cup walnuts
- 1 teaspoon ground nutmeg
- 1 teaspoon vanilla extract

## DIRECTIONS

1. Preheat oven to 325°F, and in the meantime take the baking sheet and line it with parchment paper.
2. Grind the walnuts in a food processor and keep pulsing until they are well ground.
3. Add the vanilla extract, erythritol, nutmeg and coconut flour to the ground walnuts in the food processer. Pulse again until all the ingredients are blended.
4. Put butter in the food processer in the form of small pieces and pulse until you get a soft and smooth mixture.
5. Make 16 balls on the baking sheet with the help of a cookie scooper and use your hands to press them to give them a cookie shape.
6. Place in the preheated oven and bake for 15 minutes or until you find the cookies well baked.
7. Remove from the oven once baked, set them aside for 15-20 minutes to cool.
8. Sprinkle some additional nutmeg over the delicious walnut cookies if you like before you serve them.

## NUTRITION

- Calories: 340
- Fat: 26g
- Carbohydrates: 3g
- Protein: 19g

# 193. CHOCOLATE CAKE WITH VANILLA GLAZE

## INGREDIENTS

- ½ cup almond flour
- 4 tbsp butter
- 3 tbsp stevia powder
- 5 large egg yolks
- 1 tsp agar powder
- ½ tsp salt
- 2 tbsp cocoa powder
- 1 tsp chocolate extract, unsweetened

**For the glaze:**
- 1 cup Mascarpone cheese
- 5 large egg whites
- 2 tbsp swerve
- 2 tsp vanilla extract
- Dark chocolate chips, optional

## DIRECTIONS

1. Plug in the instant pot and pour 1 cup of water in the stainless-steel insert. Line a fitting springform pan with some parchment paper and set aside.
2. In a large mixing bowl, combine egg yolks and butter. Beat with a hand mixer for 2-3 minutes, or until well combined. Add stevia, agar powder, salt, and cocoa, Beat again for 2 minutes. Finally, add almond flour and beat again until fully combined.
3. Pour the mixture in the springform pan and gently flatten the surface with a spatula.
4. Set the trivet on the bottom of your pot and place the pan on the top. Close the lid and adjust the steam release handle. Press the "Manual" button and set the timer for 40 minutes. Cook on "High" pressure.
5. Meanwhile, combine all glaze ingredients and remaining egg whites in a large mixing bowl. Beat until well combined and set aside.
6. When you hear the cooker's end signal, perform a quick pressure release and open the pot. Transfer the pan to a wire rack and let it cool for 10 minutes.
7. Top the cake with glaze and spread evenly. Add ½ cup of water to the pot and return the pan on top of the trivet. Close the lid and adjust the steam release handle. Cook for 1 minutes on the "Manual" mode.
8. When done, perform a quick pressure release and open the pot.
9. Chill to a room temperature and refrigerate for 20 minutes before serving.
10. Optionally, top with some dark chocolate chips for some extra flavor.

## NUTRITION

- Calories: 263
- Total Fats: 21.5g
- Net Carbs: 3.6g

- Protein: 12.3g
- Fiber: 1.6g

**PREPARATION: 20 MIN**

**COOKING: 30 MIN**

**SERVES: 5**

# 194. RUM TRUFFLES

## INGREDIENTS

- ½ cup dark chocolate chips, melted
- 1 cup heavy cream
- ¼ cup granulated stevia
- ¼ tsp xanthan gum
- 3 egg yolks
- ½ cup whipped cream

**Spices:**
- ½ tsp rum extract
- ¼ tsp cinnamon, ground
- ½ tsp stevia powder

## DIRECTIONS

1. In a mixing bowl, combine egg yolks, granulated stevia, and xanthan gum. Using a hand mixer, beat until well incorporated. Add heavy cream, melted chocolate chips, rum extract, cinnamon, and stevia powder. Beat for 1 more minute and then pour into oven-safe ramekins. Wrap the top of each ramekin with aluminum foil and set aside.
2. Plug in your instant pot and pour 1 cup of water in the stainless-steel insert. Position a trivet on the bottom and place ramekins on top. Close the lid and adjust the steam release handle. Press the "Manual" button and set the timer for 30 minutes. Cook on "High" pressure.
3. When you hear the cooker's end signal, release the pressure naturally. Open the pot and top with whipped cream and powdered stevia before serving.

## NUTRITION

- Calories: 208
- Total Fats: 18.5g
- Net Carbs: 9.4g
- Protein: 3.2g
- Fiber: 0.1g

**PREPARATION: 15 MIN**

**COOKING: 45 MIN**

**SERVES: 8**

# 195. MINT CAKE

## INGREDIENTS

**For the layers:**
- 1 cup almond flour
- 1 cup coconut flour
- 1 tbsp stevia powder
- ¼ cup whole milk
- 3 tbsp butter
- 5 large eggs
- 1 tsp vanilla extract
- ½ tsp salt

**For the filling:**
- ¼ cup butter
- ½ cup cream cheese
- 2 tsp stevia powder
- 1 tsp mint extract

## DIRECTIONS

1. In a large mixing bowl, combine almond flour, coconut flour, stevia powder, and salt. Mix until combined and set aside.
2. In a separate bowl, combine eggs, butter, milk, and vanilla extract. Using a hand mixer, beat until fluffy and then gradually add to dry ingredients. Mix until all well incorporated. Set aside.
3. In another bowl, combine all filling ingredients. With a paddle attachment on, beat until well combined and set aside.
4. Pour 1 cup of water in the stainless steel of your instant pot. Line a fitting springform pan with some parchment paper. Set the trivet on the bottom of the pot and place the pan on top. Pour half of the layer mixture in the pan and close the lid. Adjust the steam release handle and press the "Manual" button. Set the timer for 20 minutes and cook on "High" pressure
5. When you hear the cooker's end signal, perform a quick pressure release and open the pot. Transfer the layer to a wire rack to cool. Repeat the process with the remaining mixture.
6. When the second layer is done, spread the filling over and top with the remaining layer. Close the lid of your pot and adjust the steam release handle. Press the "Manual" button and set the timer for 5 minutes on "High" pressure.
7. When done, perform a quick pressure release and open the pot.
8. Chill to a room temperature before serving and optionally, garnish with some fresh mint.

## NUTRITION

- Calories: 398
- Total Fats: 33.8g
- Net Carbs: 6.6g
- Protein: 10.5g
- Fiber: 7.5g

**PREPARATION: 5 MIN**

**COOKING: 10 MIN**

**SERVES: 2**

# 196. VANILLA CHERRY PANNA COTTA

## INGREDIENTS

**For the vanilla layer:**
- 1 cup heavy whipping cream
- 2 tbsp whole milk
- 1 tsp agar powder
- ½ tsp vanilla extract
- 1 tbsp walnuts, roughly chopped

**For the cherry layer:**
- 1 cup heavy whipping cream
- 1 tsp agar powder
- 1 tbsp almonds, roughly chopped
- 2 tsp cherry extract

## DIRECTIONS

1. Plug in the instant pot and combine all vanilla layer ingredients in the stainless-steel insert. Press the "Saute" button and stir constantly. Bring it to a light simmer and then press "Cancel" button. Transfer to a large bowl and set aside.
2. Clean the pot and pat-dry with a kitchen paper. Now, add all cherry layer ingredients and stir well. Again, bring it to a light simmer, stirring constantly.
3. Pour about ½-inch thick vanilla layer in a medium-sized glass. Now, add the second layer of the cherry mixture. Repeat the process until you have used both mixtures.
4. Optionally, garnish with some fresh mint and refrigerate for at least 1 hour before serving.

## NUTRITION

- Calories: 467
- Total Fats: 48.7g
- Net Carbs: 4.6g

- Protein: 4.5g
- Fiber: 0.8g

**PREPARATION: 5 MIN**

**COOKING: 15 MIN**

**SERVES: 10**

# 197. KETO BERRY PANCAKES

## INGREDIENTS

- ½ cup almond flour
- 4 pieces large eggs
- 4 ounces cream cheese (softened)
- 1 teaspoon lemon zest
- 1 tablespoon butter (for frying)
- 1 tablespoon butter (for topping)
- ½ cup of frozen berries

## DIRECTIONS

1. In a mixing bowl, put in almond flour, eggs, cream cheese, and lemon zest. Whisk until the batter is well combined.
2. In a skillet over medium heat, melt the butter for frying.
3. Scoop about 3 tablespoons of batter and pour it on the skillet. Cook the pancake for about 2 minutes or until it turns golden.
4. Flip the pancake to its other side and cook it for another 2 minutes.
5. Transfer the cooked pancake to a plate. Continue cooking the rest of the batter.
6. Serve the pancakes topped with berries.

## NUTRITION

- Calories: 110
- Carbs: 2g
- Fats: 10g
- Proteins: 4g
- Fiber: 1g

**PREPARATION: 10 MIN**

**COOKING: 15 MIN**

**SERVES: 4**

# 198. MOCHA POTS DE CRÈME

## INGREDIENTS

- 2 large eggs, separated
- 1 cup coconut milk, full-fat
- ¾ cup heavy cream
- 2 tbsp cocoa powder, unsweetened
- 3 tbsp brewed espresso
- 3 tbsp stevia powder

**Spices:**
- ¼ tsp salt
- 1 tsp vanilla extract

## DIRECTIONS

1. In a small bowl, whisk together eggs, cocoa powder, espresso, stevia powder, vanilla, and salt. Set aside.
2. Plug in the instant pot and press the "Saute" button. Pour in the coconut milk and heavy cream. Give it a good stir and warm up.
3. Press the "Cancel" button and slowly pour the warm milk mixture over the egg mixture, whisking constantly.
4. Divide the mixture between 4 ramekins and loosely cover with aluminum foil.
5. Position a trivet at the bottom of your pot and pour in 2 cups of water. Gently place the ramekins on top and seal the lid.
6. Set the steam release handle to the "Sealing" position and press the "Manual" button.
7. Cook for 15 minutes.
8. When done, perform a quick pressure release and open the lid. Remove the ramekins and transfer to a wire rack. Cool to a room temperature and then refrigerate for about an hour.

## NUTRITION

- Calories 257
- Total Fats: 25.5g
- Net Carbs: 3.5g
- Protein: 5.5g
- Fiber: 2.1g

**PREPARATION: 15 MIN**

**COOKING: 30 MIN**

**SERVES: 8**

# 199. LEMON CAKE WITH BERRY SYRUP

## INGREDIENTS

**For the cake:**
- 3 cups almond flour
- 3 tbsp stevia powder
- ¼ cup coconut milk, full-fat
- 1 tbsp coconut cream
- ¼ cup butter, softened
- 5 large eggs
- ¼ tsp salt
- 3 tsp baking powder
- 2 tsp lemon extract

**For the syrup:**
- ¼ cup raspberries
- ¼ cup blueberries
- 1 tbsp lemon juice, freshly squeeze
- ¼ cup granulated stevia

## DIRECTIONS

1. In a large mixing bowl, combine together almond flour, stevia powder, baking powder, and salt.
2. Mix well and add eggs, one at the time, beating constantly.
3. Now add coconut milk, coconut cream, butter, and lemon extract. Using a paddle attachment beat for 3 minutes on medium speed.
4. Grease a small cake pan with some oil and line with parchment paper. Pour the mixture in it and tightly wrap with aluminum foil.
5. Plug in the instant pot and set the trivet at the bottom of the inner pot. Place the cake pan on top and pour in one cup of water.
6. Seal the lid and set the steam release handle to the "Sealing" position. Press the "Manual" button and cook for 25 minutes.
7. When done, perform a quick pressure release and open the lid. Carefully remove the pan and set aside.
8. Now press the "Saute" button. Add berries and pour in one cup of water and granulated stevia. Gently simmer for 5-6 minutes, stirring constantly.
9. Finally, add agar powder and give it a good stir. Cook until the mixture thickens.
10. Pour the syrup over chilled cake and refrigerate for 2 hours before serving.

## NUTRITION

- Calories: 186
- Total Fats: 16g
- Net Carbs: 3.8g
- Protein: 6.4g
- Fiber: 1.3g

# 200. KETO FROSTY

## INGREDIENTS

- 1 ½ cups heavy whipping cream
- 2 tablespoons cocoa powder (unsweetened)
- 3 tablespoons Swerve
- 1 teaspoon pure vanilla extract
- Salt to taste

## DIRECTIONS

1. In a bowl, combine all the ingredients.
2. Use a hand mixer and beat until you see stiff peaks forming.
3. Place the mixture in a Ziploc bag.
4. Freeze for 35 minutes.
5. Serve in bowls or dishes.

## NUTRITION

- Calories: 164
- Total Fat: 17g
- Saturated Fat: 10.6g
- Cholesterol: 62mg
- Sodium: 56mg
- Total Carbohydrate: 2.9g
- Dietary Fiber: 0.8g
- Total Sugars: 0.2g
- Protein: 1.4g
- Potassium: 103mg

# 201. EASY RUM CHEESECAKE

## INGREDIENTS

- 2 cups almond flour
- 4 large eggs, separated
- ¼ cup coconut cream
- 2 tbsp almond butter
- ¼ cup cocoa powder, unsweetened
- ¼ cup swerve
- 3 tsp baking powder
- 3 cups Mascarpone
- 1 cup plain Greek yogurt
- 2-3 drops stevia

**Spices:**
- 2 tsp rum extract
- ½ tsp cinnamon powder

## DIRECTIONS

1. Plug in the instant pot and position a trivet. Pour in one cup of water in the stainless-steel insert and set aside.
2. Beat egg whites and swerve with a hand mixer until light foam appears. Add egg yolks, coconut cream, almond butter, baking powder, and cocoa powder, beating constantly.
3. Finally, add almond flour and continue to beat until completely combined.
4. Pour the mixture into lightly greased cake pan and cook for 15 minutes on the "Manual" mode.
5. When done, perform a quick pressure release and open the lid. Remove the cake from the pan and cool for a while.
6. Now combine Mascarpone and Greek yogurt. Add rum extract, cinnamon powder, and stevia. Using a hand mixer, mix well until completely combined.
7. Pour the mixture over the crust and refrigerate for a couple of hours before slicing.

## NUTRITION

- Calories 247
- Total Fats: 18.1g
- Net Carbs: 5.6g
- Protein: 15.6g
- Fiber: 1.7g

# 202. SWEET AND SOUR SAUCE

## INGREDIENTS

- Apple cider vinegar
- 1⁄2 tablespoon tomato paste
- A teaspoon of coconut amino acid
- Bamboo spoon
- Water treatment
- Chopped vegetables

## DIRECTIONS

1. Mix kudzu powder with five tablespoons of cold water to make a paste.
2. Then put all the other spices in the pot, then add the kudzu paste.
3. Melt coconut oil in a pan and fry onions.
4. Add green pepper, cabbage, cabbage and bean sprouts, then cook until the vegetables are tender.
5. Add pineapple and cashew nuts and mix a few times.
6. Just pour a little spice into the pot.

## NUTRITION

- Calories: 3495
- Sodium: 33mg
- Dietary Fibre: 1.4g
- Total Fat: 4.5g
- Total Carbs: 16.5g
- Protein: 1.7g

# CONCLUSION

Menopause is the natural biological process experienced by women when they stop menstruating for 12 months straight and when reproductive hormones are no longer produced by the body. This is a physically stressful period during which women undergo several bodily changes.

Weight gain is caused by several factors during menopause: hormonal fluctuations, loss of muscle mass, insulin resistance, and poor sleeping habits. Other symptoms include mood changes and hot flashes, among others. Diets to correct hormonal imbalances and reduce discomfort are prescribed by medical professionals. One of the recommended diets for menopausal women is the well-known ketogenic diet, which is a low-carb, high-fat diet.

The ketogenic diet has been highly praised for the benefits of weight loss. This high-fat, low-carb diet has been shown to be extremely healthy overall. It really makes your body burn fat, like a talking machine. Public figures appreciate it too.

A ketogenic diet is not only beneficial for weight loss, but it also helps improve your overall health in a positive way, even if you are not a menopausal woman. Unlike all other diet plans, which focus on reducing calorie intake, ketogenic focuses on putting your body in a natural metabolic state, that is, ketosis. When you eat a lot of fat and protein and significantly reduce carbohydrates, your body adjusts and converts the fat and protein, as well as the fat that it has stored, into ketones for energy. This metabolic process is called ketosis. This is where the ketogenic diet comes from.

Printed in Great Britain
by Amazon